A LAW
FOR THE LION

April 2004
For Fernando Gutiérrez,
with best wishes,
Beatriz de la Garza

NUMBER ELEVEN
Jack and Doris Smothers Series in Texas History, Life, and Culture

A Law for

A TALE OF CRIME AND INJUSTICE

University of Texas Press, Austin

the Lion

IN THE BORDERLANDS

Beatriz de la Garza

Publication of this work was made possible in part by support from the J. E. Smothers, Sr., Memorial Foundation and the National Endowment for the Humanities.

Copyright © 2003 by Beatriz de la Garza

All rights reserved

Printed in the United States of America

First edition, 2003

Requests for permission to reproduce material from this work should be sent to Permissions, University of Texas Press, P.O. Box 7819, Austin, TX 78713-7819.

♾ The paper used in this book meets the minimum requirements of ANSI/NISO Z39.48-1992 (R1997) (Permanence of Paper).

LIBRARY OF CONGRESS CATALOGING-IN-PUBLICATION DATA

De La Garza, Beatriz Eugenia.
  A law for the lion : a tale of crime and injustice in the borderlands / Beatriz de la Garza. — 1st ed.
     p.   cm.—(Jack and Doris Smothers series in Texas history, life, and culture ; no. 11)
Includes bibliographical references and index.
  ISBN 0-292-71614-1 (cloth : alk. paper)—ISBN 0-292-70189-6 (pbk. : alk. paper)
  1. Trials (Murder)—Texas—Laredo. 2. Mexican Americans—Texas—Laredo—Social conditions. 3. Texas, South—Social conditions. I. Title. II. Series.
  HV6534.L37 D4 2003
  364.15′23′09764462—dc21

                             2002156530

*One law
for the lion
and the ox
is oppression.*

—WILLIAM BLAKE

CONTENTS

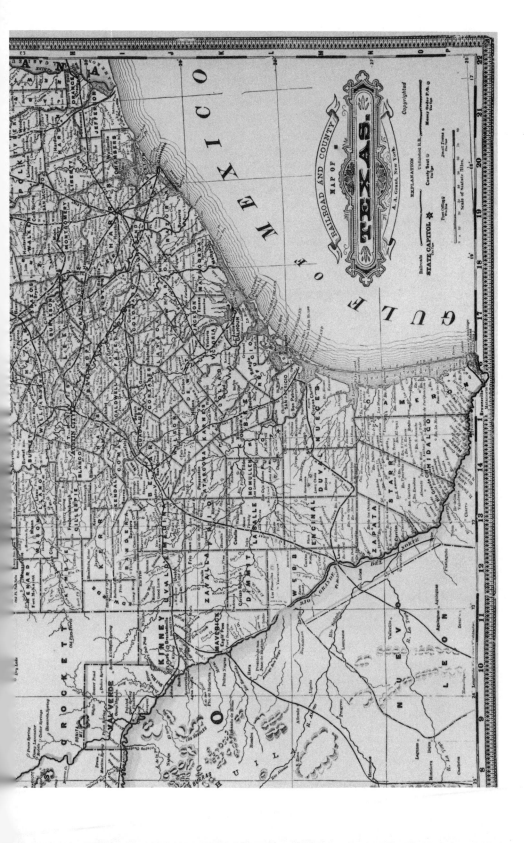

TEXAS.

RAILROAD AND COUNTY

MAP OF

A. A. Grant, New York.

Copyrighted

EXPLANATION

Railroads

Unfinished R.R. ....

State Capitol ☆ ...... One Star

County Seat ⊙ .... Two Stars

Money Order P.O. ⊙ .... One Star

Post Office ○ .... Two Stars

Scale of Sixteen Miles.

Francisco Gutiérrez Garza and his wife, Manuela García, circa
1900. (Courtesy Mrs. Sylvia Lozano Trzaskoma)

PREVIOUS PAGE: South Texas counties and railroad lines, circa
1890. (Courtesy Mrs. J. Conrad Dunagan)

Manuel Gutiérrez García at
his wedding in 1895. (Courtesy
Mrs. Sylvia Lozano Trzaskoma)

Francisca Peña, twenty-two years
old, at her wedding to Manuel
Gutiérrez in 1895. (Courtesy
Mrs. Sylvia Lozano Trzaskoma)

Boys' school in Ciudad Guerrero, Tamaulipas, Mexico, circa 1910, where
Francisco Gutiérrez Peña studied before his family moved to Laredo. (From
the author's collection)

Double funeral procession for Francisco Gutiérrez and his son, Manuel Gutiérrez, August 16, 1912. (Courtesy Mrs. Sylvia Lozano Trzaskoma)

Group of mourners and horse-drawn hearses at Gutiérrez funeral. (Courtesy Mrs. Sylvia Lozano Trzaskoma)

Francisco Gutiérrez Peña, oldest son of Manuel Gutiérrez and Francisca Peña, circa 1916, at eighteen. (From the author's collection)

Virginia Gutiérrez, oldest child of Manuel Gutiérrez and Francisca Peña, in 1914 at eighteen years of age. (From the author's collection)

Francisca Peña, Viuda de Gutiérrez, with one of her children, circa 1920. (From the author's collection)

Street scene showing the *Laredo Daily Times* offices, circa 1910. (Courtesy Laredo Public Library, Laredo, Texas)

Webb County Courthouse, constructed in 1909. (Courtesy Webb County Heritage Foundation)

District Attorney John Anthony Valls.
(Courtesy Webb County Heritage
Foundation)

ABOVE RIGHT: District Judge John F.
Mullally. (Courtesy Webb County Heritage Foundation)

Webb County sheriff Amador Sánchez,
circa 1907. (Courtesy Texas State
Library and Archives Commission)

Justice of the Peace Nicasio Idar (center) with his sons, Clemente (left) and Eduardo (right), 1907. (Courtesy Mr. Ed Idar, Jr.)

District Attorney John Anthony Valls in his office, circa 1935. (Courtesy Laredo Public Library, Laredo, Texas)

The newsroom of the *Laredo Daily Times* in March 1913. Jim Falvella is on the left, Justo S. Penn on the right. (Courtesy Webb County Heritage Foundation)

Justo Sabor Penn, publisher of the
Laredo Times, when he was a member
of the Texas Legislature in 1910.
(Courtesy State Preservation Board,
Austin, Texas)

Defense attorney Marshall Hicks,
circa 1920. (Courtesy Texas State
Library and Archives Commission)

Part I

AUGUST 1912

It was still early August, and the maximum temperature readings at the Fort McIntosh weather station on the banks of the Rio Grande hovered between 104 and 105 degrees Fahrenheit, but the people of Laredo, Texas, and the surrounding border area had begun to anticipate the end of the dog days of summer. The trains arriving in Laredo were brimming with passengers who, perhaps optimistically, had already concluded their summer vacations. On Saturday, August 10, for example, the *Laredo Daily Times* reported that Mrs. Justo S. Penn, wife of the publisher of the *Times,* and her children had returned from a three-week visit to friends in Bustamante, Nuevo León, in northern Mexico. Bustamante is located at the edge of the Sierra de Bustamante, at a higher altitude than Laredo—no doubt the reason why the Penn family chose the spot to escape the worst of the border summer (Municipios 78). Bustamante was also on the railway line between Laredo and Monterrey, Mexico's most important northern city.

And whereas Mrs. Penn (née Alicia Herrera) traveled north on the tenth of August, a few days later, on Wednesday, August 14, the *Laredo Daily Times* reported the presence, en route to Mexico City, of Gustavo Madero, Mexico's finance minister, who had spent several weeks in Galveston, Texas, "enjoying life at the seaside." In hindsight, Gustavo Madero's sojourn by the sea may appear like fiddling while Mexico burned, for even then, in the summer of 1912, his brother, the president of Mexico, Francisco I. Madero, was battling insurrection from Emiliano Zapata in the south and from Pascual Orozco in the north, as the *Daily Times* also reported in various issues spanning August 9 to August 15. However, the *Laredo Daily Times* apparently missed the opportunity to interview Gustavo Madero, since no mention is made of any comments made by him during his stopover. This omission might have been due to the absence of the newspaper's editor and publisher, who had left for San Antonio on the day before. Justo S. (Justo Sabor, born James Saunders) Penn had traveled on the International and Great Northern Railway on Tuesday, August 13, accompanied by Webb County Sheriff Amador Sánchez, to attend the State Democratic Convention held in San Antonio. Both were delegates from Webb County, according to the *Daily Times.*

Laredo in 1912 was well served by the railroads. Four lines had had depots there since the 1880s. The International and Great Northern was "one of the principal feeders to Jay Gould's great southwest system [and had] its southern terminus at the foot of Eagle Pass street [where it had] built large and commodious freight and passenger depots, besides round and coach houses," according to a pamphlet published in 1889 by the Laredo Immigration Society (Tarver 9). Coming from the other direction, the Mexican National Railroad had its northernmost terminus in Laredo, a distance of 837 miles from Mexico City. According to the same promotional pamphlet of the Immigration Society, the Mexican Railroad had built in Laredo "one of the largest, most elegant and costly depot buildings in the state. . . . It is equipped with palatial sleeping and dining cars, and its scheduled passenger time between Laredo and the City of Mexico will be 36 hours" (Tarver 10).

Travelers coming from Mexico City to Laredo on the Mexican Railroad could continue north on the I&GN, as the International and Great Northern was known, to Saint Louis, Missouri, via San Antonio, stopping along the way at little settlements such as Webb that had sprung up as railroad towns between Laredo and San Antonio (Green, *Overview* 13). Or they could travel east from Laredo toward Corpus Christi and the Texas Gulf Coast on the Texas-Mexican Railroad, passing Tex-Mex railroad towns such as Aguilares, which had started out as a Mexican *ranchería* in the early nineteenth century (*Shared* 67). Up the river from Laredo, railway service was provided by the Rio Grande Eagle Pass Railroad, which traversed a distance of some twenty-five miles to the Santo Tomás mines (Green, *Overview* 16).

But downriver from Laredo, connections with the sister settlements founded by Don José de Escandón in the middle of the eighteenth century—Revilla (later renamed Ciudad Guerrero), Mier, Camargo, and Reynosa—still depended on the state of the dirt cart roads and on the flood stages of the Rio Grande, since they were all across the river in Mexico.

Revilla, of the Escandón settlements the closest to Laredo in both distance and age, had produced the seed—some would say the flower— of many of Laredo's prominent families. Of these Laredo families it was often said that they were of Guerrero and Laredo, because their ancestral homes had been built in Guerrero when it was still called Revilla and when both banks of the river were in the same country. The situation of the family of Don Francisco Gutiérrez Garza was typical of the border area. Don Francisco and his wife, Manuela García de Gutiérrez, lived in Ciudad Guerrero, but their son, Manuel, and their daughter, Adela, lived in Laredo with their respective spouses and children. It is not clear at what point or points Manuel and Adela had moved to Laredo, or if it had been done gradually or as a sudden event precipitated by the political upheaval following the Madero revolt in 1910 and the end of the thirty-year rule of President Porfirio Díaz. However, the move was a logical one, since the family ranches were in Zapata and Webb Counties.

The situation of these binational families is better understood if we remember that at the time of the settlement of this area, the Rio Grande did not divide two countries but was merely an obstacle for ranchers with lands and cattle on both sides of its banks. Francisco Gutiérrez and Manuela García had been born and grown up in Guerrero and had married and raised their family there, but the lands which they had inherited from their ancestors were on the north—or east, on that stretch of the river—side of the Rio Grande/Río Bravo, in what is now Zapata County. Don Francisco descended from the original settlers of Revilla, one of whom, Bernabé Gutiérrez, had been awarded a grant of land in 1767, the earliest date for land titles in that area.

Land titles along the Rio Grande south of Laredo originate from the General Visita of 1767, the official survey that granted lands to the settlers, known as the General Visit of the Royal Commission to the Colonies of Nuevo Santander.

> The results accomplished by this Commission are among the strongest influences left by the Spaniards in the Texas Valley and the Acts performed are, perhaps, the most far-famed events in Spanish colonial history of northern Mexico. Even descendants of primitive Spanish settlers date the beginning of time on the

Rio Grande from the "General Visita." This is not surprising when one considers that it is from this year that all Valley grants of land date their origin. (SCOTT 62)

The same historian, Florence Johnson Scott, goes on to describe the results of the actions of the commission on the settlers, particularly those in Laredo and Revilla:

The lands surrounding and opposite the original towns were included in districts known as the jurisdictions of Laredo, Revilla, Mier, Camargo and Reynosa. The Jurisdiction of Laredo included eighty-eight *porciones* [a measure of land, roughly equivalent to a league, fronting the river], although more than twenty were left vacant due to the fact that there were so few settlers there. At Revilla, which later became Guerrero, there were sixty-eight *porciones,* all of which were adjudicated; these fronted on both the Salado and the Rio Grande rivers. . . .
While practically all of the settlers lived on the south bank of the Río Grande, where they built their homes and cultivated their fields, many of them chose the *porciones* north of the river for their ranching lands. . . .
These ranchers were accustomed to cross the river in canoes, and the length of time that they were away from their families depended on the season of the year, and the amount of work to be done on the ranches. Cattle and sheep herders pro-tected their interests when they were absent. (68–70)

Jack Jackson, in *Los Mesteños,* adds this description: "The typical rancher [along the Rio Grande] either built a *casa fuerte* of stone or stayed in town, placing the ranch in the hands of a trusted *major-domo*—often a nephew, son-in-law, or other relative" (444).
After 1821 it was the government of the Republic of Mexico that made grants of land in Texas, among them the Charco Redondo Grant, awarded in 1835 to Anastacio García, Manuela García's grandfather, and located in modern-day Zapata and Jim Hogg Counties (*Guide* no. 91). In addition to inheriting her share of this property, Manuela acquired the shares of other heirs, and in this manner she and Francisco put together the Rancho San Juan, some 6,000 acres in Zapata County.
Following Texas's independence from Mexico, it was the Republic

of Texas first, and later the State of Texas, that made grants, as well as sales of land, to individuals. Francisco Gutiérrez Garza was among those individuals. Not content with merely inheriting land or buying the interests of fellow heirs, he had also begun purchasing land in Webb County made available by and through the State of Texas. Since the 1870s he had acquired sizable tracts northeast of Laredo and had continued to do so during the first decade of the twentieth century. By 1912 Don Francisco had accumulated approximately 6,000 acres in Webb County, which comprised a ranch he called La Volanta, according to the Webb County Probate Records. Manuel Gutiérrez García, his son, had also acquired some eight sections of state land (a section contains 640 acres) in Webb County, near his father, as of 1912.

With all this land, the father and the son faced the problem of the distances that separated the ranches in the two counties, as well as the distance from their home in Guerrero to the various ranches. Don Francisco's brother, Julián, and his sons had also bought several tracts in Webb County, close to their relatives. According to the 1910 census of Webb County, Julián Gutiérrez, then sixty years old, lived in Laredo with his wife, Catarina García, and their four children: Estanislao, 32; Pilar, 25; Laureano, 23; and Francisco, 17. The men listed their occupation as farm or ranch work, and Julián stated that he had immigrated (with his family, presumably) to Texas from Mexico in 1899. It was Julián and his sons, then, who most likely looked after Francisco and Manuel's land and cattle in Webb County, while Manuel and his father probably tended the property in Zapata County, making only periodic trips to La Volanta, such as for roundups and branding.

However, the situation in Webb County must not have been satisfactory to Don Francisco, even with the help of his brother and nephews, because in 1911 he leased La Volanta to A. J. Landrum of Laredo. In July of the following year, though, Manuel received the disturbing information that someone else, not Landrum, was in possession as tenant of La Volanta, and he made this fact known to his father. The discovery had upset Don Francisco to the extent that he made preparations to travel to Laredo to consult an attorney and to meet with his son there. For Don Francisco, preparing to leave Guerrero was not a simple matter. Before doing so, he was required to obtain official leave to absent himself from the municipality, since he served on the Guerrero city council or *ayuntamiento* as *alcalde primero*, a title that subsequently caused the newspapers much confusion.

Traveling from Guerrero to Laredo was no easy feat. There was no railroad that ran downriver from Laredo. The trip from Guerrero to Laredo presented two options, neither comfortable nor secure. Travelers could either cross the Río Bravo by *chalán,* or ferry, from Guerrero to Zapata and proceed from there upriver along a dirt road that was barely fit for carts, or they could follow a similarly bad road on the Mexican side of the river up to Nuevo Laredo, and there cross the river on the relatively recently built International Bridge. Of the two possibilities, the latter was probably the preferable, since the ferry crossing was always chancy, and this risky venture still had to be followed by a long and uncomfortable ride, perhaps on horseback or, at best, by cart.

As an illustration of the condition of the road from Laredo to the south, we read that, as late as 1914, the mail bound for Zapata and Laredo from downriver—and vice-versa—was carried on horseback because that was the fastest means to use on the existing road. Virgil N. Lott and Mercurio Martínez recount this process in their book, *The Kingdom of Zapata:*

> Every day, except Sunday, the canvas bags with newspapers and other small parcels and the leather pouches with letters and first-class mail arrived at Zapata late in the afternoon from down river. Here the men rested at night, but six o'clock the next morning, rain or shine, cold or hot, the mail left Zapata for San Ygnacio, where another rider, his mount saddled and ready, after receiving the mail for up-river points was off at a bound. Here the Zapata man exchanged his tired mount for a fresh horse, received the down-river mail and was back in Zapata by four in the afternoon. The up-river rider was met at Becerro Arroyo, twelve miles distant from Laredo, where he was relieved of his mail by a rider from La Posta; both men returned to their respective stations. At La Posta (exchange station), a rider from Laredo picked up the mail, relieving the La Posta man. (38)

Despite the lack of roads in the downriver communities, the Laredo business elite preferred to concentrate its efforts on road improvements to the north of the city. The *Laredo Daily Times* of August 16, 1912, carried an editorial, "For Good Roads," that urged the proposal to link Laredo with San Antonio by highway, although a rail connection already existed between the two cities. The editorial read in part: "A project is now on foot to link Laredo with San Antonio by a highway which shall . . . provide an efficient roadway for all kinds of wheeled-traffic. It is to be hoped that the citizens of Laredo will take definite action [toward] the early completion of the Laredo–San Antonio highway."

To the south, travel by automobile between Laredo and Zapata was probably possible in 1912, but just barely so. An old-time Zapata resident, Beatriz C. Izaguirre, reminisced about an automobile trip between the two locations, circa 1920:

> One day my sister, brother and I went with my father and my mother to Laredo on business. This was when there were no paved roads in Zapata County and the roads were only trails in the countryside. We had to stop the car when we saw another car coming in the opposite direction, as the roads were so narrow. The roads were also very bumpy and we had to travel very slowly. We would shake all the way even though the maximum speed was 15 to 20 miles per hour. . . . It was not only hard to drive because the roads were rough, but besides that, there were several arroyos we had to go through in order to get to Laredo. If it happened to rain that day, you could not come back the same day. The arroyos were full of water and one had to wait for the water level to subside. (IZAGUIRRE 39)

At this point we must make an educated guess and assume that Don Francisco Gutiérrez and his wife would have opted to travel from Guerrero to Laredo in August 1912 on the road that ran parallel to the river on the Mexican side. Because both river roads—on opposite sides—were on the whole equally bad, the couple would have preferred to cross the river on the International Bridge that joined both Laredos, rather than trust their luck with the more risky *chalán* from Guerrero to the settlement of Zapata (both the county and the county seat were called Zapata). Francisco and Manuela would have traveled to Nuevo Laredo, most likely by mule-drawn wagon, since automobiles were then a rarity in Guerrero, and even in Laredo horse- and mule-drawn wagons still outnumbered autos.

There is no record that Manuela accompanied her husband on this trip, but this too can be safely assumed because, barring an illness or some personal calamity, this would have been the most natural course of action. Francisco and Manuela's two children and all their grandchildren now lived in Laredo. If Francisco went through the trouble of making the problematic trip to attend to business in Laredo, then Manuela would have gone with him to visit their family.

Francisco and Manuela had had six children, but of this number only two had survived to adulthood: Manuel, the oldest, and Adela, the youngest. Adela married Ernesto Flores in Guerrero in 1900, while Manuel married Francisca Peña, also in Guerrero, in 1895, according to the marriage records of the parish of Nuestra Señora del Refugio of Guerrero, Tamaulipas. Manuel and Francisca had seven children, to whom their grandmother, Manuela, was affectionately known as "Mamelita"—a contraction of "Mamá Manuelita"—and they were eager to see her that summer.

That summer of 1912, Manuel, Francisca, and their seven children were at their San Juan Ranch, not in Laredo, so Manuela and Francisco would have stayed with their daughter. However, even if that had not been the case, Manuela would probably still have stayed with Adela when she came to Laredo. It would have been more natural for Manuela to feel more comfortable at her daughter's house than at her daughter-in-law's. But her situation was more complicated than the traditional one with tension between mother-in-law and daughter-in-law, for the two women were also first cousins, although Manuela was twenty-one years older than Francisca.

Francisca was the daughter of Juan Martín Peña and his wife, Virginia García. Manuela's parents were José María García and María Gertrudis Peña. Juan Martín Peña and Gertrudis Peña were brother and sister. Therefore, Francisca and her husband, Manuel Gutiérrez, were first cousins once removed. Although marriage between cousins was often permitted—indeed, it would have been difficult to avoid in those small communities—it was not always well received, and there appears to have been some friction between Manuela and Francisca due to this cause, according to one of Francisca's granddaughters.

The personalities of the two women may also have had something to do with any tension that existed between them. Photographs of Manuela and Francisca hint at the strong will that animated each of them. One photograph taken around 1900, of Francisco and Manuela in middle age, shows a prosperous-looking couple. As was the custom at the time, he is sitting while she stands by him, an unfurled fan in her hand. He is a broad-chested man, with a confident air in his posture and strong hands that reveal a lifetime of physical work. A steel rod seems to run down Manuela's back, the result perhaps of the corset that also produced the wasp-waist—a slender woman with a proud carriage. Her face is delicately molded, with deep-set blue eyes, but her hands, like her husband's, reveal a lifetime of work. The wedding portrait of Francisca, taken in 1895 when she was twenty-two, shows a dark-haired "proud beauty" in a white lace mantilla. Her flashing eyes, which appear dark in the photograph, were actually blue, like Manuela's. With such an attractive cousin, it was understandable that Manuel had not looked elsewhere for a wife.

Manuel's parents had put together the San Juan Ranch, in Zapata County, out of Manuela's share of the inheritance of the Charco Redondo Grant and what they had bought from other heirs. The Charco Redondo had comprised at the time it was granted in 1835 more than 22,000 acres, but with the large families that were prevalent then and the passage of several generations, individual heirs often received at most a few hundred acres (*Guide* no. 91). The San Juan Ranch encompassed more than a quarter of the original grant and required, as well as deserved, the frequent presence and direct attention of the owners. But there were only two men to oversee the approximately 17,000 acres in Webb and Zapata Counties. In addition, there was Francisca Peña's ranch, Sabino Verde, in Guerrero.

When Juan Martín Peña died in 1908, Francisca and her younger sister, Esther, had been his only heirs, since Juan Martín had been a widower for many years. The sisters had inherited adjoining ranches on the banks of the Río Sabinas, near Guerrero, which were named for the sabine trees (*sabinos*) growing along the river: Sabino Verde for Francisca and Sabino Seco for Esther. With Francisca and Manuel in Texas, the care of Sabino Verde would have fallen either to her father-in-law or to Lorenzo de la Garza, Esther's husband, since both men were in Guerrero.

The summer of 1912, then, found the Gutiérrez men concerned with the management of their lands but still able to enjoy the benefits of their comfortable position. Manuel and Francisca and their children were at the San Juan Ranch for both personal and business reasons. Even in those days when most people lived in rural areas or in small towns, it was considered healthy, particularly for children, to go to the country during the summer vacation from school. At the San Juan Ranch, Manuel and Francisca's brood, which ranged in age from fifteen to one, could run free at play and at work, *al aire libre*, breathing in the fresh country air that was supposed to undo the ravages of the stuffy air in town. They could drink foaming warm milk, almost directly from the cow, and eat freshly picked fruits and vegetables.

Of course, it was not all play for the children; they were expected to help their parents, according to their age and sex. The oldest was a girl, Virginia, named after her maternal grandmother. In the early days of August 1912, Virginia was already anticipating the arrival of her sixteenth birthday on August 22. Soon after that she would be returning to the Ursuline Convent School in Laredo, where she was to begin her senior year. Virginia had been a boarding student at the Ursuline Convent while her parents were living in Guerrero, but now she could enjoy her school days while enjoying the warmth of living with her family as well.

Virginia, Manuela García's oldest grandchild, was already a budding beauty and undoubtedly her grandmother's favorite. It is quite probable that it was Manuela who paid for Virginia's schooling with the Ursulines. But although surrounded by affection, Virginia would not have led a pampered existence, particularly at the ranch. She and her thirteen-year-old sister, Adelina, would have been expected to help their mother with the domestic chores, at the very least caring for the younger children.

For fourteen-year-old Francisco, the oldest boy, summertime would have been devoted to helping his father and the ranch hands with their work. For the men, summer was the time to carry out improvements on the land, when fences and corrals were built or mended, dams reinforced, and wells dug. Lorenzo de la Garza's family, for example, would repair to their ranch, Sabino Seco, in the summer months, as he related to his son in a letter dated May 17, 1922: "Yo pienso ir por los meses de julio y agosto a pasar las vacaciones en el rancho y ver que trabajo realizo estando allá la familia" ("I plan to spend the vacation months of July and August at the ranch and see what work I can accomplish while the family is there").

The family, even the young children, would all have been involved in harvesting the produce from the cultivated plots, such as beans, corn, squash, and melons, which augmented the usual diet of meat, milk, cheese, eggs, and tortillas, both corn and flour. The women and the girls, however, would always be careful to wear sunbonnets and long-sleeved garments to protect their complexions from the sun. Those summers at the ranch were a happy time for the families along the border, idyllic in many ways but never idle.

However, according to one of Virginia's daughters, when young Virginia learned in early August that her father was preparing to go to Laredo to meet her grandfather, she was ready to return to the city. She wanted to see her grandparents, perhaps spend her birthday with them. She particularly wanted to visit with her doting grandmother, for she had no other. Her maternal grandmother and namesake, Virginia García, had died at the age of twenty-nine, leaving two orphaned little girls, Francisca and Esther, and her oldest grandchild knew her only from photographs.

But Manuel Gutiérrez refused to allow his daughter to accompany him to Laredo. Perhaps he was too preoccupied with the business at hand, the reason for the trip, to view the occasion as a happy family gathering. The situation at La Volanta was a worrying one and required serious deliberation. According to the lease that Don Francisco had made with A. J. Landrum in May 1911, which was to run until May 1915, Landrum was to make quarterly rent payments in advance. Presumably Landrum made the payments throughout 1911 and at the beginning of 1912. However, it appears that the lease payment due on April 1, 1912, was not made.

Don Francisco does not seem to have taken any immediate action on the missed payment. Perhaps he was willing to be accommodating because A. J. Landrum appeared to be a respectable family man. The *San Antonio Express* had reported on Sunday, July 7, 1912, on the wedding of one of Landrum's daughters in Laredo: "A pretty wedding took place at the home of Mr. and Mrs. A. J. Landrum, 1814 Victoria Street . . . when one of the pretty daughters of the home, Miss Bessie Landrum, became the bride of Charles Virgil Kyle of San Antonio."

Don Francisco and his son did become concerned when a check for $450.26 was forwarded by Ernesto Flores, Adela's husband, to Manuel at Aguilares, Texas, a settlement on the Texas-Mexican Railway and the closest post office to the San Juan Ranch. The check was drawn on the Stockmen's National Bank of Cotulla, Texas, and was dated July 6, 1912. It was made payable to Manuel Gutiérrez (not Francisco) and was signed by Alonzo W. Allee with the notation "Six month lease April 1 to October 1."

Manuel communicated this change in the state of affairs to his father in Guerrero. Don Francisco then made plans to go to Laredo and asked his son to meet him there. The lease with Landrum had been drafted by a lawyer. It was typewritten and in a legal format, using legal terminology. The lawyer is not identified, but in the recent past—in 1909—when the right of Don Francisco and Manuel to hold the land they had purchased from the State of Texas had been challenged by the state itself, they had turned to E. A. Attlee, a member of the long-established firm of Attlee and Attlee of Laredo and a former mayor of the city, for help in responding to the state. It is possible, then, even probable, that it was Attlee who prepared the lease for Don Francisco in 1911. One curious detail of this lease is that it was witnessed by T. C. Mann, one of the attorneys who later prosecuted Alonzo Allee. We can infer from this detail that T. C. Mann was either the attorney who prepared the lease—a somewhat unorthodox, not to say unethical, procedure if he was both attorney and witness—or, more likely, an associate of Attlee and Attlee.

Regardless of the authorship of the 1911 lease, Don Francisco and Manuel turned again to a lawyer in August 1912, or at least to a scrivener, who made the necessary changes—such as substituting Alonzo Allee's name (which was spelled "Alonso" Allee) for A. J. Landrum's— but retained the same basic terms, such as rental payments, in the new lease. There is an intriguing clue as to the authorship of this lease in the spelling of the lessee's name: the scrivener wrote *Alonso,* which is the Spanish form of Alonzo W. Allee's name, which may lead us to think that the scrivener's first language was Spanish. *Alonso* was also the name of one of Manuel's children. This document, unlike the earlier lease, is handwritten in beautiful script, such as lawyers, lawyers' clerks, and educated persons used then. The change from mechanical to manual writing is not significant in itself, though, since legal documents were drafted in either form at that time, as a perusal of courthouse records shows.

Armed with this new lease, Don Francisco and Manuel set out for La Volanta, in northeast Webb County, to have the document signed by the new man in possession, Alonzo W. Allee. We do not know if Don Francisco—or Manuel—was familiar with the Texas law regarding subleases, or if either was acquainted with the terms under which Landrum had transferred his lease to Allee. Normally, leases are assignable or transferable to third parties under the principles that govern the Anglo-American law of property:

> All leases, except leases at will [which this was not], may be
> assigned provided there is no restriction in the lease itself [there

was not; the lease refers to "Landrum and his representatives and assigns"]. A leasehold interest in real estate is personal property and is transferable as such. Although a leasehold is personal property (a chattel real), it is also an interest in land and transfers must comply with the Statute of Frauds. Thus, if the assigned lease has more than one year to run, the transfer must be in writing in order to be enforceable [footnote omitted]. By an assignment, the tenant conveys all of his interest in the property to a third person for the entire term, whereas in a sublease the tenant conveys all or part of his interest for a period less than the entire term.   (CRIBBET 219)

However, under Article 5489 of the *Revised Civil Statutes of Texas* (1911), a tenant was not permitted to sublet without the landlord's consent. The law in question read:

If lands or tenements are rented by the landlord to any person or persons, such person or persons renting said lands or tenements shall not rent or lease said lands or tenements during the term of said lease to any other person without first obtaining the consent of the landlord, his agent or attorney.

We do not know if Landrum had assigned his interest to Allee or merely sublet La Volanta to him, or even if he had simply abandoned the lease, a possibility that cannot be discounted since Landrum seems to have missed the April and July payments in 1912. What seems clear is that Landrum had not obtained Don Francisco's permission to sublet La Volanta, and therefore Allee was a trespasser at La Volanta, without a lease to govern his presence or his status. In fact, Landrum had already breached the terms of his lease by failing to make the quarterly payments of $225.13 each due on April 1 and July 1. Allee's payment of $450.26, which he made on July 6, purported to relate back to April and extended until October, but it is doubtful that this payment cured the breach. It is also unclear whether in making this late payment Allee was acting as Landrum's assignee or as his representative under the terms of the lease, or even if such lease terms were effective in light of Article 5489.

This is not the time or place for an in-depth discussion of the fascinating ramifications of the property doctrine known as adverse possession, which has played an important role in landownership in Texas. Suffice it to say that adverse possession was very probably a major concern with Don Francisco Gutiérrez and his son when contemplating the presence of Alonzo Allee on their property. The relevant Texas statute in effect at the time was Article 5681 of the *Civil Statutes*, enacted in 1879, but according to the Texas Supreme Court in *Houston Oil Company of Texas v. Jones*, 109 Tex. 89, decided in 1917, the concept was an older one.

The court began by quoting the statutory definition of adverse possession: "Adverse possession is an actual and visible appropriation of the land, commenced and continued under a claim of right inconsistent and hostile to the claim of another." However, the court continued, the concept of adverse possession had already been propounded, even before the enactment of the statute, in 1875 in the case of *Word v. Droughett*, 44 Texas 365. In *Word* the court had held that the adverse claimant's entry upon the land must have been "with the intent to claim it as his own or to hold it for himself [citations omitted]" (Woodward and Hobbs 195).

It must be reiterated here that adverse possession was the legally sanctioned means by which individuals without title to land acquired not only possession of the land but also title to it, to the detriment of the legal owner. From the point of view of Don Francisco Gutiérrez, Alonzo Allee might be tendering a lease payment and thus behaving like a tenant and not an adverse claimant, but that was now. Who could foresee what he would do in the future, particularly since his presence at La Volanta was not governed by an enforceable lease?

The suspicion that Alonzo Allee's presence might be undesirable was not based solely on legal questions, nor was it entirely unfounded or unreasonable, although it might have been a case of the sins of the father being visited on the son. There appears to have been nothing known against Alonzo Allee around 1912, but it was an entirely different case with his father, Alfred Y. Allee, who, by most counts, had killed five men before he himself succumbed to a violent death at the hands of the Laredo city marshal, Joe Barthelow, in August 1896 (Ludeman 116–117).

Don Francisco and Manuel Gutiérrez, however, did not go see Alonzo Allee expecting violence, for they were not proposing to evict him from La Volanta. They were primarily concerned with the status of the lease. That was the reason for drafting a new document, inserting Allee's name as the new lessee. The Gutiérrez men wanted to clarify the situation, so that in the future there would be no ambiguities that could be resolved in favor of an adverse claimant. There should have been no reason for Alonzo W. Allee to resort to violence—but he did.

Newspapers often have trouble keeping all the facts straight. The *Laredo Daily Times* knew that a double killing made for a big story, and it reported the main facts of the occurrence accurately, but it got lost somewhat in the whos and whys. On Thursday, August 15, 1912, the *Daily Times* carried on the front page the headline TWO PROMINENT MEN KILLED: MAYOR OF GUERRERO AND HIS SON, PROMINENT RANCHMEN OF THIS COUNTY, KILLED BY ALONZO ALLEE.

It may surprise contemporary newspaper readers, accustomed to the ubiquitous qualifier "alleged," to note the refreshingly forthright manner in which the *Daily Times* identified the killer. However, the facts did seem to point to one conclusion: if three men had been alone in a room, and two were dead from gunshot wounds while the third was missing, the third man must have been the killer.

The *Laredo Daily Times* was an afternoon paper, and although the news of the tragedy reached the paper on the evening of the day of the killings, it was too late for that day's edition, as the story explained: "Yesterday evening, shortly after six o'clock, the sheriff's department received telephone advice from Encinal announcing that a double tragedy had been perpetrated at "El Alamito" ranch, a distance of 45 miles from Laredo in the northeast corner of Webb County and about 25 miles from Encinal."

A perplexing detail of the story is the reference to the place of the killing as El Alamito, when in all references to the land by Don Francisco or his representatives it was known as La Volanta. It is common, though, for ranches, like towns, to take their names from some prominent landmark in the vicinity. There was a creek in Webb County known as Alamitos Creek—*alamitos,* or little cottonwood trees, probably grew along it—which crossed some of Don Francisco's land. "El Alamito" may have been the old name of a ranch in the area, perhaps comprising part of the land that Don Francisco bought, and the name may have persisted among old-time settlers even after Don Francisco renamed it. "La Volanta" is a rather fanciful name meaning, according to the *Diccionario de la lengua española* of the Real Academia, "coche de las Antillas," a coach or carriage used in the Antilles. The locals may have been more comfortable with a ranch named after a creek or a tree than after something unfamiliar, and the name carried to the newspaper story.

The report from the *Daily Times* continued:

> The dead men are Francisco Gutiérrez, mayor of the town of Guerrero, Mexico, and owner of the ranch where the tragedy occurred, and his son, Manuel Gutiérrez, a citizen of Laredo, and one of the most prominent ranch men and land owners of this county. The man who did the killing was Alonzo Allee, lessee of the ranch. The killing of Gutiérrez and his son occurred yesterday forenoon at about 11 o'clock, and the delay in getting the information here was by reason of the fact that a courier had to ride to Encinal, 25 miles distant, to telephone the officers in Laredo.

The first thing that strikes one on reading this paragraph is the prominence that the *Laredo Daily Times* accords to the dead men. Of course, the eminence of the victims makes the story more newsworthy, but a perusal of other Texas English-language newspapers of that era finds few Mexicans mentioned at all, and when they are, the term "bandit" is usually appended to their names. The *Brownsville Herald* provides a sampling of the headlines of the era: ALLEGED LEADER IN BANDIT TROUBLES CHARGED . . . WITH HORSETHEFT: ONE OF THE INDICTMENTS WAS AGAINST LUIS DE LA ROSA, ALLEGED BANDIT LEADER (March 18, 1916), as well as RANGER TIMBERLAKE KILLED BY MEXICAN BANDIT (October 11, 1918). And even the *Laredo Daily Times* contributed this in 1913, referring to Gregorio Cortez, the hero of the eponymous border ballad: NOTED CRIMINAL PARDONED (July 23, 1913).

What is perhaps even more surprising than the attention the Laredo paper devoted to the killing is the fact that the story was also carried by the San Antonio newspapers. Obviously, the San Antonio press covered the border area to the extent of having a correspondent, or at least a stringer, in Laredo, and thus by Thursday, August 15, the day after the killing, the *San Antonio Light* carried the story, although much abbreviated:

RANCH MEN MURDERED
Sheriff's Posse Searching for Slayers in Webb County

Francisco Gutierrez and his son, Manuel, prominent ranch men and landowners in the northeastern part of Webb County, 45 miles from here [Laredo], were murdered yesterday. The details are not known. A sheriff's posse in automobiles is looking for a young man believed to be connected with the crime.

The correspondent is circumspect as to the details, but the story assumes that a crime had been committed and that it had been a murder. It also refers to "slayers" in the plural, most likely because there was more than one victim, although the sheriff's posse is reported to be looking for only one young man, without naming Alonzo Allee.

It was not until Friday, August 16, that the *San Antonio Express* reported the story: TWO RANCH OWNERS DEAD: FRANCISCO AND MANUEL GUTIERREZ SHOT AT EL ALAMITO RANCH; ALONZO ALLEE, LESSEE, SURRENDERS.

The story, which had arrived by "Special Telegram" to the *Express*, related the facts of the killing and repeated the *Laredo Daily Times*'s identification of Francisco Gutiérrez, saying: "The elder Gutierrez was also mayor of the town of Guerrero, Mexico, and owner of the ranch and was at the ranch on a visit with his son."

It would have been a matter of common knowledge, at least among journalists in South Texas, that under the old Spanish law which until the 1820s had governed from California to Patagonia, the office of *alcalde* referred to the highest civil authority at the local level. However, the law had changed somewhat under the Mexican Republic, and local governing councils, or *ayuntamientos*, were now organized in a different fashion. They were directly elected by the voters, for one thing. In the spring of 1912, Francisco Gutiérrez Garza had been elected to the *ayuntamiento* of Ciudad Guerrero, Tamaulipas, Mexico, as *alcalde primero*, the first in rank of three such officials, but he was not the mayor.

Under the new municipal government scheme in effect in 1912, the chief executive of a municipality was (and still is) the *presidente municipal*. The Municipal Archives of Nueva Ciudad Guerrero, Tamaulipas, Mexico, contain the election results of the local election of 1912. The new municipal council consisted of the *presidente municipal*, Jesús García Benavides; seven *regidores* (aldermen), Juan García Martínez, Dr. Isidoro A. Nava, Antonio Ma. Benavides, Santiago Gutiérrez, Alfredo González, Juan B. Benavides, and Régulo Flores; two *síndicos* (municipal attorneys or prosecutors), Refugio Peña and José Ma. Salinas;

three *alcaldes propietarios,* the first being Francisco Gutiérrez Garza, and the other two Lorenzo González and Reyes Gutiérrez; and three *alcaldes suplentes,* or alternates, Lucio Vidaurri, Diego Martínez, and Manuel Firons. As an interesting aside, we may note here that the jurisdiction known in Mexico as a municipality combines the functions of city and county government, so that the Municipality of Ciudad Guerrero, Tamaulipas, consisted not only of the city of Guerrero but also of several small communities. One of these communities was known as La Leona, where the voters in the municipal election of 1912 numbered twenty-seven, all of whom voted in favor of Francisco Gutiérrez Garza for *alcalde primero.*

Under Spanish and Spanish American law, *alcaldes* had exercised mostly a judicial function (Escriche 417). However, along the border the term *alcalde* came to be synonymous with "mayor." Thus the title and office that were attributed to Don Francisco in the newspapers are understandable. The municipal scheme of government under which Don Francisco was elected, though, had evolved after Mexico's independence from Spain had been consolidated in 1821. Escriche's *Diccionario razonado de legislación y jurisprudencia* describes the type of municipal government that existed in Mexico in the nineteenth century and explains that a certain latitude was permissible in the composition of the *ayuntamientos:*

> El Ayuntamiento de Méjico se componía de seis alcaldes, diez y seis regidores, y dos síndicos con la denominación de 10. y 20.; pero el artículo 23 de la 6a. ley constit. dice: "El número de alcaldes, regidores y síndicos se fijará por las juntas departamentales respectivas, de acuerdo con el gobernador, sin que puedan exceder los primeros de seis, los segundos de doce y los últimos dos." [The Mexico City Council was composed of six alcaldes, sixteen aldermen, and two prosecutors; but Article 23 of the 6th constitutional law says: "The number of alcaldes, aldermen, and prosecutors shall be set by the respective departmental governing bodies, in accord with the governor; however, these may not exceed six in the first instance, twelve in the second, and two for the last."]   (ESCRICHE 344)

The function of the *alcalde primero,* Francisco Gutiérrez Garza's office, was more notarial than judicial. In May 1912, for example, Francisco Gutiérrez Garza's signature appears attesting to the execution of a deed of gift by which Francisca Salinas, Viuda de Salinas, a widow, conveyed the title to a house to her daughter. Earlier, in 1909, Don Francisco, as *alcalde primero*, was one of those attesting to the protocol of the intestacy proceedings in the Estates of Juan Martín Peña and Virginia García, the deceased parents of his daughter-in-law, Francisca Peña.

It is interesting to follow just a little longer the trail of mistranslations of the term *alcalde* in the stories of the killings of Francisco and Manuel Gutiérrez. On Saturday, August 17, we find the Spanish-language Laredo weekly paper, *El Demócrata Fronterizo* (which should have known better), carrying the story along the same lines as the English publications but adding its own brand of misinformation. The writer of *El Demócrata* knew that the office of mayor was equivalent in Mexican municipal government to the office of *presidente municipal.* This writer did not bother to find out the exact office that Don Francisco held in Guerrero, and relying instead on the stories from the *Laredo Daily Times,* he converted Don Francisco into the *presidente municipal* of Guerrero as he proceeded to relate the story of the killings:

> Gran consternación causó en esta ciudad la noticia circulada el miércoles, de que en la mañana de ese día habían sido muertos en su rancho, cerca del Encinal, el Sr. Francisco Gutiérrez García [sic] y su hijo Manuel por un individuo de apellido Allee que tenía en arrendamiento un terreno de los Srs. Gutiérrez.
>
> Don Francisco era Presidente Municipal de C. Guerrero, Tamaulipas, y había venido, con licencia del Gobierno, al arreglo de algunos asuntos particulares.
>
> [The news circulated in this city on Wednesday that Mr. Francisco Gutiérrez García [sic] and his son, Manuel, had been killed on their ranch near Encinal caused great consternation. The killer is an individual named Allee who had leased the Gutiérrez land.
>
> Don Francisco was the municipal president of Guerrero, Tamaulipas, and had come here, with leave from the government, to take care of some personal business matters.]

Returning to the *Laredo Daily Times* story of the killings, we can infer from its second paragraph that the courier who had ridden his horse for twenty-five miles to Encinal to notify the authorities of the crime had either been a witness to the killings or was carrying a message from one who had been. However, this important character who rode twenty-five miles through the *chaparral*, the low, thorny brush that lined the rough *senderos*, or trails, down into gullies and washes and up rocky hills, was never identified by the newspaper. That the subsequent legal proceedings connected with the killings revealed the identity of this crucial personage is almost a certainty, but the reader of the *Times*, with no other source of information, would have been left in the dark as to his identity, as we have been.

The *Laredo Daily Times* continued relating the events of August 14:

> Immediately upon receipt of the intelligence of the killing, officers made preparations to go to the scene of the tragedy, and at 10 o'clock last night three automobiles left for "El Alamito," one of them containing Deputy Sheriffs Stoner and McKenzie and Justice Idar, and the other two having aboard Undertaker Convery and several relatives of the dead men from this city. They reached the ranch at an early hour this morning and after taking charge of the remains started back to this city and arrived here this afternoon.

Today, at the dawn of the twenty-first century, we have become accustomed to instant communications and to traversing miles in minutes. A century ago Laredoans already felt greatly liberated from the physical constraints of time and space, for, after all, they had had the telegraph and the railroads for some time, and now they even had long-distance telephone; but they still lacked good roads. It took the courier on horseback several hours to travel twenty-five miles through the brush to Encinal, and it took the automobiles sent to retrieve the bodies some six or seven hours to reach the scene of the crime, a distance of forty-five miles from Laredo.

This observation raises the question of how Francisco and Manuel Gutiérrez had traveled to El Alamito/La Volanta. We have no information as to this, so we are forced to fall back on reasonable inferences. They could have ridden on horseback, although the distance of forty-five miles, which may or may not have been according to the flight of the proverbial crow, would have certainly put a strain on both horses and riders. Or they could have traveled by mule-drawn wagon, a common means of transportation in the country, but the wagon and the mule team required more of a road than a single horse did, which could have imposed a more circuitous route, such as the one that the automobiles must have followed.

The two men could have also utilized a combination of transport that involved both horses and train, as their killer did when he arrived in Laredo. According to the *Times*, "After the killing Allee evidently left the ranch, for he arrived at Webb [the I&GN railway station north of Laredo] this morning and surrendered himself to Deputy Sheriff J. E. Hill, who arrived here with him on the train this afternoon."

The Gutiérrez men could have taken the train from Laredo to Webb, where they would have been met with fresh horses by Don Francisco's nephews, whose ranch adjoined La Volanta. Again, we have no evidence that this is what happened. We only have the newspaper's vague description of the events leading up to the tragedy, but the scenario described above seems the most likely under the circumstances. The *Daily Times* described the events in this manner:

> Francisco Gutierrez, who owns the ranch and is the mayor of Guerrero, Mexico, arrived here [Laredo] several days ago, having secured a leave of absence from his official duties in Guerrero. Here he met his son, Manuel, who is a resident of Laredo, but who had been spending vacation time on the ranch with his wife and seven children, and who had come to Laredo to meet his father and accompany him to the ranch. Last week both left here together for the ranch and had been there ever since on a business visit. Besides owning considerable valuable property in this county, the deceased were owners of ranches in Zapata County.

The newspaper story makes it sound as if Manuel and his family had been staying at their ranch in the northeast corner of Webb County, and we have seen earlier that this was not so. They had been staying at the San Juan Ranch in Zapata County, as the letter from Ernesto Flores to Manuel Gutiérrez, enclosing Allee's lease payment, clearly shows. The letter was forwarded to Manuel in Aguilares, Texas, which, although also in Webb County, is in the extreme southeastern part of it, near the Zapata (and now also Jim Hogg) county line, in the direction of the San Juan Ranch, from which Manuel went to Laredo to meet his father.

It is understandable that the Gutiérrez men would have spent sev-

eral days inspecting their Webb County properties, as the newspaper relates, because Manuel Gutiérrez owned over 5,000 acres there, separate
from his father's, which were not included in the Landrum lease and
where he probably ran some cattle. But family relations also dictated an
extended visit, not to mention that a ninety-mile round trip across the
brush country was not a matter for a single day. Don Francisco's brother,
Julián, and his sons owned a ranch, Los Cantaritos (a *cántaro* is a little
water jug), which was located about a mile from La Volanta. The only
course of action for Don Francisco and his son when visiting La Volanta
was to stay at Los Cantaritos, especially since La Volanta was occupied
by a dubious tenant.

Familial feelings also made it unthinkable for Don Francisco
not to stay with his brother, so, although the newspaper referred to the
visit as a "business visit," family and business were one and the same.
Ranching was the family business, and Don Francisco could count on
his brother to look after all the Gutiérrez lands because they were all engaged in a common family enterprise. Acquiring the land in Webb
County had certainly been a family enterprise, begun under the leader-
ship of Francisco Gutiérrez Garza.

It was in 1875 that Francisco, then only thirty-three years of age,
first bought Land Scrip No. 1/321, issued by the General Land Office of
Texas to Beaty, Seale & Forward under the Act to Improve Navigation of
the Sabine, Neches and Angelina Rivers and Pine Island Bayou. The land
scrip represented 640 acres of land, and the seller was Meyer M. Levy,
who may have received it from Beaty, Seale & Forward as repayment of
a loan or as payment for services or supplies, since land scrip was used
in place of money by both the State of Texas and the railroad and improvement companies.

The ability of the Republic of Texas first, and the State of Texas
later, to pay for public works with land was unique in the country,
Thomas Lloyd Miller tells us in *The Public Lands of Texas, 1519–1970:*

> In the development of its transportation system, Texas had an
> advantage over others of the United States. Texas had a bounti-
> ful public domain which could be bestowed on those who would
> contribute to provide a transportation system. The land was
> given to encourage river and harbor improvements, to foster ship
> construction, to promote the digging of canals, and to subsidize
> the construction of roads and railroads. (70)

The act under which Beaty, Seale & Forward was compensated for waterways improvements was approved on April 29, 1874, and it was one of many such legislative acts passed in the 1870s. According to Miller, "[B]eginning in 1873 and continuing until 1879, Texas went through a veritable 'canal and ditch craze'" (72). Under the April 29, 1874, act, Beaty, Seale & Forward received 1,175,680 acres of land for cleaning, clearing, and improving the rivers targeted in the act (Miller 287–288).

The companies receiving the land as payment for improvements had no use for most of it and disposed of the scrip as quickly as possible. That was how Meyer M. Levy, by L. G. Levy, his attorney in fact, of Nueces County, Texas, conveyed to Francisco Gutiérrez Land Scrip No. 1/321, corresponding to 640 acres of land, "for and in consideration of one hundred dollars," according to the document of sale found in the archives of the General Land Office of Texas. Land Scrip No. 1/321 represented Survey number 479 in what was then Encinal County and which became the eastern part of Webb County when it was incorporated into it in 1899. Survey 479 was the "home section" of Francisco Gutiérrez's ranch where the original improvements, including a dwelling, were located, the land which allowed him to purchase additional acreage directly from the State of Texas. Survey 479 was also, most likely, the site of the murder of Francisco and Manuel Gutiérrez.

Francisco Gutiérrez was not the only inhabitant of Guerrero, Tamaulipas, to acquire lands in Texas in the 1870s. Besides his brother, Julián Gutiérrez, and his sons, who also settled in Webb County, there is at least one other instance of this kind of land purchase in Zapata County that is included in the *Texas Family Land Heritage Registry.* In 1875 two brothers from Guerrero, Leonardo and Teodoro Treviño, settled on land purchased by their father from Stone, Kyle and Kyle, land scrip issued for water transportation improvements. The Treviño brothers began in this manner their land acquisitions in Zapata County, where they first raised sheep and later cattle (*Texas Family,* 83–84).

What prompted this northward expansion by the people of Guerrero is not clear. However, the end of the war against the French, which concluded with the execution of the Emperor Maximilian in 1867, and the beginning of a long stretch of peace, lasting—with a few interruptions—until 1910, must have made for a feeling of optimism among the people of the northern frontier of Mexico and propelled the more venturesome border residents to extend their ranching activities north of the Rio Grande. Of course, another important factor in this northward movement was the fact that land was readily available in Texas, having been put into circulation as currency by the state, while in northern Mexico land holdings had shrunk since the 1700s as families, in multiplying, had had to divide their properties.

However, this northern expansion was not without its problems, as the killings of Francisco and Manuel Gutiérrez show. In going north of Laredo and farther away from the border to establish new ranches, Francisco and Manuel Gutiérrez very possibly incurred the displeasure of the Anglo landowners who had begun to move south of the Nueces River in the years following the Civil War, and particularly after the arrival of the railroads to Laredo in the early 1880s:

> The economy [of Webb County] began to change in the 1880s, however, with the arrival of the railroads. . . . The construction of the rail lines brought jobs for the work crews and also made it easier for ranchers to ship livestock to market and to receive manufactured goods from the East and Midwest.
>
> The connection with the outside world also had far-reaching effects on the culture of the county, for it brought an infusion of American culture to what had been essentially a Mexican ranching community. After 1881 the number of Anglo-Americans began to increase, and by 1900 they represented one fourth of the population of 21,851.   (LEFFLER AND LONG 6:865)

The tensions that developed between newly arrived Anglos and the established Mexican ranchers may provide an explanation for what is otherwise a riddle with an unsatisfactory answer. Unless we look behind the reported facts, the conduct of the killer remains a puzzle. The *Laredo Daily Times* reporter, writing on August 15, voiced the same frustration at not being able to recount more than the bare facts and next to nothing of the motivation:

> While the *Times* reporter has made every possible effort to glean full information of matters leading up to the killing, every effort has proven futile. After his arrival at the jail here Mr. Allee was reticent and had nothing to say in this connection. However, it is believed by some that the killing was the result of some dispute over land matters or in connection with the lease of the ranch, but this surmise cannot be sustained.

Alonzo Allee was certainly exercising his right to silence while in custody, reserving his statement until he had been advised by legal counsel. In the meantime, all that the *Times* reporter could garner in the way of additional information was comments made by Justice of the Peace Nicasio Idar after holding a coroner's inquest on the two deaths. The *Times* reported on August 15:

> Justice Idar and Deputy Sheriffs Stoner and McKenzie returned this afternoon about 2:15 o'clock. From Justice Idar, who held an inquest on the bodies and took what evidence he could get, the *Times* reporter got a meager account. Justice Idar stated that there was only one witness to testify. The witness stated that he was nearby when Allee and the two men became involved in a quarrel and some hot words passed, then a shot rang out and the witness took flight. What ensued in the killing of the two men, the witness could not tell. That is all the evidence the coroner could get, hence the details are very meager.

Justice Idar, like Allee, was reticent with his comments, not wanting to jeopardize the prosecution's case, just as Allee undoubtedly did not want to make his lawyer's job more difficult by making unwise admissions.

On Friday, August 16, the *Laredo Daily Times* carried the story of the double funeral of Francisco and Manuel Gutiérrez on page 3. The headline called attention to this unusual feature of the tragedy: FU-NERAL THIS MORNING: VICTIMS OF DOUBLE TRAGEDY INTERRED TODAY; PROCESSION BEING A LARGE ONE. The text went on to expound:

> The first double funeral witnessed in Laredo in a number of years took place from San Agustin Cathedral this morning at 9 o'clock to the Catholic cemetery, when the remains of Fran-cisco Gutierrez and his son, Manuel Gutierrez, who were killed at "El Alamito" ranch on Wednesday by Alonzo Allee were con-veyed to their resting place.

The persistent *Times* reporter writing this series of stories was, most likely, Jim Falvella, who was on the staff of the newspaper dur-ing the first decades of the twentieth century and who, with his photo-graphs of Laredo scenes, left a valuable pictorial record of the area and the era. It was probably Falvella who took the photographs of the double funeral procession. Falvella (assuming he was the reporter) persevered in his pursuit of the story of the Gutiérrez killings and brought off a minor scoop by describing for his readers, in the same story, the condition of the bodies of the victims which he had garnered from his own observations (although he denied this) and also from interviews with the undertaker, John Convery:

> Shortly after the arrival of the bodies here yesterday quite a crowd gathered about the undertaking parlor, but none viewed the remains until they had been prepared. Judging from the appearances of the bodies, both men met instant deaths, the elder Gutierrez being shot through the center of the heart with a 45-calibre ball, while the son was shot through the back and also through the heart, according to the information given the *Times* reporter.

That was how matters stood on Friday, August 16, 1912. Don Francisco Gutiérrez Garza was dead at seventy years of age from a 45-calibre bullet to the heart, together with his son, Manuel Gutiérrez García, aged forty-two, also shot through the heart and *through the back*. They were conveyed to their final resting place in two black hearses, the first drawn by a pair of glossy bays, the second by a team of white horses. Photographs show a lengthy funeral cortege following the hearses on foot. The mourners, all men, are clad in dark coats and ties in spite of the blazing August heat. A variety of headgear, from jaunty straw boaters to sober homburgs and dark derbies, and even the occasional ranch sombrero, shielded them from the punishing sun. No women appeared in the procession since, according to custom, the women were spared the hardship of the long walk along the dusty road to the cemetery, as well as the intensely emotional moments of the last farewells.

Manuela García, a widow of sixty who had now buried five of the six children she had borne, and her cousin and daughter-in-law, Francisca Peña, a widow at only thirty-nine and with seven children, remained at home, behind the closed doors and drawn curtains of a house in mourning.

Virginia, Manuel's eldest child and Don Francisco's first grandchild, could now only look to her sixteenth birthday, less than a week away, with sorrow and anxiety. The plans for her upcoming senior year at the Ursuline convent school were thrown into disarray. Without the two men to run the ranches, the family's financial situation looked frightfully uncertain. Virginia would later tell her own children that there had been no money to pay for her convent school tuition or for her to continue her education at all, and instead, she was forced to leave home and go to work as a teacher in a country school to help out her family.

Fourteen-year-old Francisco, the second of Manuel's children, was now the man of the house and the chief mourner in the funeral procession. He was a small, slightly built young man with a serious, even anxious, expression. He had reason to be both, for now he felt the responsibility of carrying on his father's business and of looking after his mother and six brothers and sisters, the youngest of whom were too young to realize the tragedy that had befallen their family.

The day after the funeral was Saturday, August 17. After four days in San Antonio, attending the State Democratic Party convention, Webb County Sheriff Amador Sánchez and Justo S. Penn, publisher of the *Laredo Daily Times*, returned to Laredo on the International and Great Northern line. Both men had been absent from Laredo during the critical three days from August 14 to August 16 when one of the city's major crime stories of the year had unfolded, although the deputies of both men had carried on as best as they could.

Also traveling to Laredo from San Antonio on that Saturday, after also attending the Democratic Party convention, was the Honorable Marshall Hicks. The *Laredo Daily Times* of August 17 reported the return of Sheriff Sánchez and of its publisher, Penn, and added, separately: "Hon. Marshall Hicks of San Antonio arrived in the city this morning on business." Marshall Hicks could claim the title "Honorable" for several reasons. He had been present at the creation, in 1891, of the Forty-ninth Judicial District of Texas, whose seat was Laredo, by virtue of being appointed its first district attorney by then governor James Hogg. Hicks had remained in that office until 1895, when he had moved to San Antonio to open his private practice of law. In 1899 he was elected mayor of San Antonio and remained in that office until 1903 when he resigned to become a state senator. He served in that capacity until 1907 (Wharton 17). Hicks counted among his friends and patrons a former law partner, Robert U. Culberson, brother of United States Senator

Charles A. Culberson, and former Texas governors Oran M. Roberts and James S. Hogg, whose student and law clerk he had been ("Who's Who in Texas").

Now Marshall Hicks was traveling to Laredo on Saturday, August 17, on business. Marshall Hicks had a client in the Webb County jail waiting to consult with him before he talked to anyone else. The client's name was Alonzo W. Allee.

Part II

A MATTER
FOR WEAPONS

Alonzo W. Allee remained in the Webb County jail until August 24, when he was freed on bail. In the ten days or so that he sat in his cell, Allee may have had time to reflect that a scant five months before, in mid-March, James Compton had been hanged within the walls of the same jail. Jerry Thompson, in his book, *Laredo: A Pictorial History*, tells us that James Barney Compton was a drifter and sometime switchman for the International and Great Northern Railroad who, together with Lonnie A. Franks, a gambler, planned and carried out the robbery and murder of a Laredo jeweler, G. J. Levytansky, in December 1911. Although the men had acted in concert, it was apparently Compton who bludgeoned and stabbed Levytansky to death. The men then divided the spoils, consisting mainly of diamonds and some money. Franks then left town and went to San Antonio, but Compton remained in Laredo, perhaps because he was in love with a "local beauty, Delia Johnson," whom he hoped to marry (252).

Compton soon became a suspect and was arrested, but he refused to confess and was released. However, when his accomplice, Franks, was arrested in San Antonio, Franks did spill the beans to the sheriff there. When he was confronted with Franks's confession, Compton broke his silence (he had been arrested again), and each man then tried to pin the blame on the other, hoping to receive a favorable deal that would spare his life. Compton, anxious to avoid a death sentence, asked District Attorney John A. Valls what his punishment would be if he confessed. Valls, being less than candid, replied that "he would do everything possible to save his [Compton's] life and that it was conceivable that he could get off with second degree murder, which carried a punishment of from five to twenty-five years in the penitentiary" (Thompson 254).

On January 5, 1912, Thompson tells us, Franks was returned to Laredo from San Antonio under heavy guard:

> A large, angry crowd had gathered at the depot awaiting his [Franks's] arrival. To avoid any possible trouble, he was taken off the train at a crossing one mile north of town and placed in an open car. Guarded by Rangers, who galloped alongside on horseback, he was escorted to the county jail. Here, however, another large crowd, "anxious to get a glimpse" of the murderer, had gathered. As the car slowed in front of the jail, the crowd pushed forward and surrounded the automobile. The Rangers "made a charge to clear the crowd," and Franks was rushed inside.   (254)

No such angry crowd had threatened Alonzo Allee when he had arrived in Laredo on the train, escorted only by Deputy Sheriff J. E. Hill, on his way to the county jail. This subdued reaction to Allee's arrest might have been due to the fact that, unlike Compton and Franks, who were drifters with few if any local connections, Alonzo W. Allee had grown up in South Texas and had been for many years in the employ— and under the protection, we can surmise—of John R. Blocker, one of the biggest ranchers in the area. In the words of his son, A. Y. Allee, who went on to become a captain in the Texas Rangers, his father, Alonzo W. Allee, "went to work for the well-known rancher, John Blocker, on the Chupadero ranch" as far back as 1896, when Alonzo Allee was only eighteen (Pattie, "A. Y. Allee" 42).

Another son of Alonzo Allee, Warren Allee, who for forty years was a field inspector for the Texas and Southwestern Cattle Raisers Association, repeated this assertion: "My father, Lonnie Allee, was working for Blocker and Combes on a ranch on the Rio Grande before he and my mother . . . married" (Pattie, "To the Letter" 100).

A historian, Gilberto Miguel Hinojosa, describes the retinue of cowboy-guards that big ranchers maintained toward the end of the nineteenth century and their effect: "The pattern of violence had already been set by some big ranchers, who maintained virtual standing armies and used them along with capital and entrepreneurship to expand their holdings" (115). Alonzo Allee seems to have fit the pattern, not so much of a life-long servitor of Blocker, but rather more of a semi-independent contractor who was standing by on call for when he was needed.

Lonnie Allee was a local boy who had influential friends in the Anglo ranching community of South Texas, people he had known since boyhood. For example, a historian of LaSalle County describes a county fair on Labor Day, 1900, in Cotulla, the county seat, complete with barbecue and rodeo events. According to this writer, there were twelve participants in the roping contest, among them "Lonnie Allee and Jack Hill" (Ludeman 34). Jack Hill became one of the leading ranchers in the community of Webb (Green, *Overview* 13). He was the selfsame Deputy Sheriff J. E. Hill who accompanied Alonzo Allee to Laredo and the county jail. When Allee left the Gutiérrez ranch after killing the two men, it was to Webb that he fled. Allee seems to have gone there not so much to turn himself in as to seek advice from a friendly lawman, his boyhood companion Deputy Sheriff Jack Hill.

Alonzo Allee was also the recipient, and in some ways the beneficiary, of the legacy left by his father, Alfred Y. Allee, a man useful as well as deadly with a gun. It is interesting to note that much more is known about Alfred Allee's exploits than about his son's. These exploits of Alfred, related by chroniclers who were openly sympathetic to him, are chilling to read today. Frank H. Bushick, writing in 1934, in his book wistfully titled *Glamorous Days*, relates the life of Alfred Y. Allee in the chapter titled "Vigilantes and Desperadoes:"

> Alfred Allee, who lived in the wildest part of LaSalle county, gained for himself the reputation of being a fearless and dangerous man. He was born in DeWitt County [Texas], May 31, 1855, but lived and ranched in Karnes County up to 1882.
>
> In those days whiskey and six shooters were part of a man's appurtenances. Allee attended a country dance near the village of Runge and became involved with a man named Word and killed him. For this he was tried and acquitted in the courthouse at the old county seat of Helena, but as new settlers began to move in and crowd up the country about that time, Allee gathered up his little stock of cattle, about five hundred head, and moved over to LaSalle county further west.   (254–255)

Five hundred head of cattle could be considered a "little stock" only in comparison to, say, five thousand; and the amount of land required to pasture five hundred head of cattle is not negligible. It is a rule of thumb among South Texas ranchers that, under the best of circumstances, it takes a minimum of 20 acres of brushland to support one cow, assuming that the land is unimproved—that is, not cleared and planted in grass—and most of the brushland in South Texas was unimproved in the late nineteenth century. Under this premise, Alfred Allee would have needed at least 10,000 acres of brushland to pasture his cattle. However, the chroniclers of Alfred Allee's life, among whom were his grandsons, make no mention of Allee owning any land or any ranch in particular.

When Manuel Gutiérrez purchased land in Webb County from the State of Texas in 1904, the land was priced at one dollar per acre and the purchase price was paid in installments. Assuming that in the 1880s, when Alfred Allee moved to LaSalle County, contiguous to Webb, the price of land was half as much as what Manuel Gutiérrez had paid, Allee would have had to pay five thousand dollars for the land he needed to pasture his five hundred head of cattle. In passing, we can also note that the ratio of 20 acres to one animal is bolstered by the Inventory of the Estate of Francisco Gutiérrez Garza (found in the Webb County Probate Records), which lists, among other property, 6,060 acres of land in the San Juan Ranch in Zapata County and two hundred head of cattle, which works out to be 30 acres per head.

Since there is no mention of Alfred Allee buying land, and if he was not likely to have had sufficient money to buy it, then if we are to believe the story of the five hundred head of cattle, we must conclude that Allee leased the land from someone or pastured his cattle on someone else's land under some other arrangement. This arrangement could have been something similar to sharecropping in farming, with a person agreeing to look after the landowner's cattle in exchange for being allowed to also run cattle of his own. We have no evidence that Alfred Allee entered into such an arrangement, and if he did we still would not know who the landowner was, but a plausible candidate for this role would have been the powerful rancher John Blocker, the subsequent employer of Alonzo Allee, Alfred's son.

The fact that Alonzo Allee went to work for Blocker after his (Alonzo's) father's death in 1896 strengthens the contention that Alfred owned no land but rented or used somebody else's. In the aftermath of the killings of Francisco and Manuel Gutiérrez, fourteen-year-old

Francisco Gutiérrez Peña, Manuel's son, was put in charge of the San Juan Ranch in Zapata County. But when Alfred Allee was killed, his eighteen-year-old son, Alonzo, went to work for John Blocker at the Chupadero Ranch.

This incident in Alonzo's employment may also be indicative of a prior acquaintance or of an employer-employee relationship between Blocker and Alfred. It is also interesting that Alonzo Allee was usually referred to in the newspapers as a "stockman," while John Blocker and Francisco and Manuel Gutiérrez were described as "ranchmen." This may seem to us today an overly subtle distinction, but in a ranching community a hundred years ago it marked the difference between those who owned both land and cattle and those who owned only the cattle, the livestock, not the land, or who looked after livestock for others, that is, whose use of land was itinerant rather than fixed.

Of course, the five hundred head of cattle may have been apocryphal, and Alfred Allee may have simply been a hired hand of John Blocker. This alternative supposition finds some support in the words of Alfred's grandson and namesake, Alfred Y. Allee (or A. Y., as he was known), who recounted that in 1901, five years after the death of the first Alfred, Alonzo had accumulated ninety-nine cows and one bull (a large herd for only one bull!). Had he not inherited, then, the offspring of his father's herd of five hundred? His only sibling was a sister, so his share of the inheritance would not have been small (Pattie, "A. Y." 43).

But even if Alonzo Allee did not inherit land or cattle from his father, he did inherit something else: a similar approach to resolving conflicts. In determining how to conduct himself as a grown man, Alonzo Allee probably had no other example than that of his father. The story of Alfred Y. Allee, as related by his chroniclers, bears being quoted at length, not only for the facts that it recounts, which may shed light on Alonzo's own actions, but, just as important, for the undertone of admiration that can be detected running throughout the narratives. This admiration stemmed in part from the fear that Alfred Allee inspired in many of his contemporaries, a fear that translated into respect in some quarters.

Bushick, the author of *Glamorous Days*, picks up the tale of Alfred Allee after he left Karnes County and moved to LaSalle: "In 1886 he [Alfred Allee] and a Frio County stockman named Frank Rhodes had an altercation on the streets of Pearsall and Rhodes was shot and killed, for which Allee was indicted, tried and acquitted" (255).

The man who had killed at least twice, although successfully preserving the presumption of innocence with his acquittals, was then hired by "the law" to put an end to the career of bank robber and highway man Brack Cornett. Alfred's grandson A. Y. Allee gave an interviewer this version of his grandfather's foray into law enforcement:

> When notorious Brack Cornett and his gang of bank and train robbers moved into South Texas in 1888 [Alfred] Allee was appointed deputy sheriff. Learning of Cornett's whereabouts he went to apprehend the outlaw and had to outshoot him instead. His proficiency with a weapon placed him on the Special Ranger list, and he was ready to ride when called.   (PATTIE, "A. Y." 43)

There is no record in the Texas State Archives of Alfred Allee ever having been appointed a Ranger, Special or otherwise. However, Alfred Allee may indeed have been deputized by the county sheriff in order to legitimate the killing of Cornett, since apprehending him was probably not a priority. Walter Prescott Webb, in *The Texas Rangers*, describes a practice of the 1920s that could have been utilized just as easily in the 1880s or 1890s:

> The Texas bankers had become exasperated at the numerous robberies that were being committed, and equally impatient with the failure of the courts to convict or to punish the robbers. Consequently, they adopted strong measures designed to rid the country of bank robbers and to save the delay and expense incident to court trials. In every member bank large placards were posted which read as follows: REWARD/FIVE THOUSAND DOLLARS FOR DEAD BANK ROBBERS/NOT ONE CENT FOR LIVE ONES.   (533)

What Alfred's grandson failed to mention about his grandfather's role in the Cornett killing was that Alfred Allee collected a reward of $3,800 that an express company had offered for Cornett's capture, "dead or alive" (Ludeman 117).

The author of *Glamorous Days* also gives a different account of Cornett's death from that given by Alfred's grandson. In this version, Cornett went to seek shelter with his friend, Alfred Allee, and instead found death:

He [Cornett] intended to make his escape and get out to Arizona, but on his way stopped to hide out and rest a few days at the Allee ranch in LaSalle county. He and Allee had been raised in the same part of the country and knew each other well. He showed up in Allee's camp one morning at breakfast time, but instead of extending hospitality, as the story goes, Allee attempted to arrest Cornett and in an exchange of shots, Allee killed Cornett.   (BUSHICK 256)

The next victim of Alfred Allee did not give him any other reason to kill him except that he, the victim, displeased Allee: "Alfred Allee boarded a train one day at Pearsall and taking offense at the manner of the negro train porter, shot and killed him," relates Bushick (256).

Another chronicler places the killing in Cotulla and describes how, when Allee was boarding the train, the "negro" porter gave him a shove, forcing him back:

As Allee was falling backwards, and before he reached the ground, he pulled his pistol and fired. No one really knows for sure but it is believed the porter was trying to stop Allee from boarding the train until the other passengers could get off. If this was the case, he used very bad judgment in shoving an armed man around. His bad judgment and lack of tact proved fatal.
                                        (LUDEMAN 117)

After reading about Alfred Allee's sanguinary exploits, it is difficult to accept the chroniclers' conclusion that all the shootings that Allee was responsible for were due to his star-crossed destiny. The relatives of the victims—and the victims themselves—would certainly have disagreed with this assessment, but those were the writers' words and, no doubt, their beliefs:

About 1892 misfortune overtook Allee once again. There were two young brothers by the name of Bowen living in Cotulla. One of them assumed the editorship of the Cotulla Ledger while the other hung out his shingle as a lawyer. There had been some criticism by the editor against Allee in the Cotulla Ledger.
                                        (LUDEMAN 117)

It was the Bowen brothers' misfortune that Allee could take no criticism and that they found themselves on the same train as Allee. According to the historian of LaSalle County, Ludeman, the brothers fired first at Allee but missed him. Allee, a better marksman, shot the lawyer, breaking his "shooting arm." He then turned on the editor and "grabbed his [Bowen's] pistol barrel with his left hand, pushed the muzzle aside, and placing the muzzle of his own gun against Bowen then fired five shots in rapid succession." According to this writer, Allee was so cold-blooded as to leave "the lifeless form of the newspaper man crumpled on top of the wounded brother." Allee then "coolly walked out of the coach, knocking the empty shells from his cartridge belt" (Ludeman 117).

Whereas it does not appear that shooting the train porter brought Allee any legal repercussions (there is no mention of an indictment or trial), the killing of Bowen the editor, and wounding of his brother the lawyer, did bring out the power of the press and the bar, and according to the same writer, Governor Hogg appointed Thomas H. Franklin as special counsel to prosecute Allee. It was to no avail. Alfred Allee hired "two fine lawyers, Hon. L. H. Browne of San Marcos and Col. E. R. Lane of San Antonio." Allee was again acquitted (Ludeman 117).

Another writer who had grown up in Karnes County hearing of Alfred Allee's exploits tells us with admiration that Allee's lawyer, the Hon. L. H. Browne, was "Judge Browne . . . formerly a citizen of this county" (Dailey 329). This writer makes no secret of his hero worship for Alfred Allee:

> Gifted, talented, a natural leader of men, it appeared as if nature had fashioned him for a statesman, and had he chosen a political career he might easily have been governor of this great state. But the "moving finger writes . . . ," and so, with all his rare gifts and friendly disposition he was continually getting into unfortunate personal difficulties. (DAILEY 326)

In the hands—or imagination—of this same biographer, the hero, Alfred Allee, had his wealth doubled and his eminence heightened. Instead of gathering five hundred head of cattle, in this version Alfred Allee "rounded up his cattle, numbering a thousand head, and moved them to Frio county, Texas, where he established a large ranch. There his herds multiplied and he prospered for many years, becoming the leading ranchman of that section and handling cattle by the thousands" (Dailey 327).

According to this same admiring chronicler, remorse over killing the unarmed train porter drove Alfred Allee to lay down his gun. This good deed turned out to be Allee's downfall. Many towns had ordinances prohibiting the carrying of firearms within the city limits, although the rule was clearly "more honored in the breach than in the observance," as a historian of the West points out: "Most of the cattle towns had laws against carrying a gun, but a majority of men were armed, anyway, frequently carrying a hidden weapon in their coat pocket" (Egloff 34).

Some lawmen, however, were serious about taming their territory. For example, in Cotulla, where Alfred Allee spent part of his adult life, the LaSalle County sheriff began a practice in 1900 of "requiring every person that came into town with a gun on . . . to check it at his office when he arrived in town. They picked up their guns when they left to go home." Along with this step, the sheriff, whose name was Will T. Hill, also convinced the state authorities to remove the Texas Rangers from Cotulla and LaSalle County, and "it was not long before Cotulla was a peaceful little village" (Ludeman 123).

Unfortunately, these attempts at eradicating gunfights came too late for Alfred Allee's victims and only too soon for Allee himself. According to both Dailey's and Ludeman's versions of Alfred Allee's death, he apparently thought it prudent to leave his gun at home when he went to Laredo in August 1896, and this civic-minded act led to his death. Dailey laments his hero's high-minded gesture:

> So his good resolution, made in the interests of humanity, instead of the reward it richly deserved, proved to be his own undoing.
> It happened in the city of Laredo on the 19th day of August, 1896. Allee is said to have gone there on business and came to an untimely end at the hands of a saloon-keeper armed with a dirk, who knew that Allee was unarmed and wished to make a great name for himself. (329)

Alfred's grandson, A. Y. Allee, told the story in a slightly different manner:

In 1896 Grandpa had some controversy with a man in Laredo. The man thought that sooner or later the situation would lead to a gun battle, and he was afraid of my grandfather, so he hid behind a saloon door and stabbed him in the back as he walked in.   (PATTIE, "A. Y." 43)

Perhaps Alfred Y. Allee the second was loath to admit that a Texas Ranger, even a putative one, would ever leave his gun at home, but the grandson makes no mention of his grandfather being unarmed when he was killed or of his having previously laid down his gun and renounced violence.

The other two versions of Alfred Allee's death bring out an additional fact, which is that Allee's killer was Joe Barthelow, the city marshal of Laredo. In *Glamorous Days* Allee's end is described in this way:

He [Alfred Allee] later went to Laredo where he expressed his intention of staying out of trouble. He was regarded as a dangerous man and was killed in a saloon there, August 19, 1896, by City Marshall Joe Barthelow. In the personal encounter Barthelow grappled Allee and almost cut his head off.   (BUSHICK 257)

There is no mention in this account of Allee having been unarmed or of his assailant attacking him from behind.

Ludeman, the LaSalle County historian, adds: "Due to Allee's reputation Barthelow got off scot-free but was later killed in San Antonio" (117).

Joe Barthelow was apparently both the city marshal and a saloon keeper, or at least associated with the beverage business through his family. The 1900 census of Webb County lists a "John Barthelow" as a "beer agent," and Falvella, in his *Souvenir Album of Laredo*, published in 1916, carries an advertisement on page 30 for "Frank Barthelow, Manufacturer of Soda Water and All Kinds of Mineral Waters. Agent San Antonio Brewing Ass'n." And if Joe Barthelow after killing Alfred Allee was himself killed in San Antonio, it happened after the Webb County elections of November 1912, because those election returns, as reported by the *Laredo Weekly Times* of November 10, 1912, list A. J. Barthelow, candidate for sheriff, as receiving one vote. Barthelow must not have been very popular as city marshal either, because he was replaced in

1898 by Michael Brennan (*Twentieth Century History* 2:106). In 1916 Falvella still listed Brennan as city marshal in his *Souvenir Album.*

Alfred Y. Allee's life and death certainly bear out the adage that he who lives by the sword dies by the sword. In this case the maxim was more figurative than actual since, although Allee did die by the sword— or at least a dagger—he had lived by the gun. Alonzo W. Allee, orphaned at eighteen, would have been expected to learn a lesson from his father's death; and, in fact, there is no known record of Alonzo Allee being involved in gunfights early on.

Alonzo Allee's first arrest appears to have been in 1912, when he was thirty-four, for killing Francisco and Manuel Gutiérrez; and here is where the lessons learned from his father's life were helpful. The most important lesson that Alonzo Allee absorbed from his father's experiences was a familiarity with the judicial process that demystified it and deprived it of the power to instill fear. Alonzo witnessed the process of his father being arrested, indicted, tried, and acquitted of killing on several occasions. The key to these favorable outcomes was, of course, to have expert legal representation. Alfred Allee had been able to call on two prominent South Texas attorneys to represent him when Governor Hogg named a special counsel to prosecute him in the Bowen killing. Now, in 1912, Alonzo Allee was able to call on three law firms to represent him: Marshall Hicks of Hicks and Teargarden of San Antonio as lead counsel, assisted by Geo. M. Martin of Atascosa County and J. Vandervoort of Carrizo Springs.

Even in those days of modest living standards almost one hundred years ago, hiring a legal defense team that included a lawyer as prominent as Hicks could not have come cheap. The question that arises with both the father's and the son's legal troubles is how they could afford to pay for legal representation on such an extravagant scale. How could simple stockmen command the services of such well-connected legal experts? The obvious conclusion is that they were not paying for it, that someone else with much more wealth and influence was responsible for procuring the legal representation for the Allee men.

We have already had a glimpse of Marshall Hicks's curriculum vitae: former district attorney of the Forty-ninth Judicial District that included Webb and Zapata Counties, former mayor of San Antonio, former state senator, friend of two governors. J. Vandervoort of Carrizo Springs was a member of a prominent Dimmit County family that included the county judge and the owners of the local title abstract company. According to Seb Wilcox, the longtime court reporter of the Forty-ninth Judicial District, F. Vandervoort had been Dimmit County's first county attorney at the time of the organization of the county in 1881 (16). Martin, the attorney from Atascosa County, was also one of the sureties that posted Alonzo Allee's initial total bond of $20,000, indicating that he was a man of means.

Someone was looking after Alonzo Allee. The identity of this benefactor does not appear anywhere, but a credible hypothesis can be put forward that it must have been someone with the influence and power of John R. Blocker—and, indeed, that it most likely was John R. Blocker, Alonzo Allee's early employer and patron. In 1907 John R. Blocker was reported to own "three ranches in Texas, one in Maverick County near Eagle Pass, another in Webb and LaSalle Counties near Encinal and another in Webb County near Laredo." He was also "interested quite heavily in an extensive cattle ranch proposition in the republic of Mexico" (*Twentieth Century History* 2:462).

Circumstantial evidence certainly places Blocker at the scene of the action. The ranch near Eagle Pass was undoubtedly the Chupadero (also called Chupadera) Ranch where Alonzo Allee went to work when he was eighteen, according to his sons. The other two ranches were in proximity to the Gutiérrez lands. Blocker had additional interests in extensive areas of land in Webb and neighboring counties. The land records of Webb County show a deed of trust (a mortgage) from Mark T. Cox et al. to John R. Blocker and H. Ford covering more than 32,000 acres in Dimmit and Webb Counties, given in exchange for a loan of $98,141.17 circa 1912.

Blocker's wealth derived from his early activities as a cattle driver:

> His [Blocker's] first trail drive was in 1873, to Ellsworth, Kansas, and from that year on until the final closing of the trail to Texas cattle, the herds of Mr. Blocker were driven annually to Kansas, Colorado, Nebraska, the Dakotas, Wyoming and Montana. In 1886 he was interested in 82,000 head of cattle on the trail at one time, and his last drive of cattle was in 1893 when he delivered 9000 head of stock to a buyer in Deadwood, South Dakota. (*History of the Cattlemen* 65)

A particularly important aspect of Blocker's biography, as related in *History of the Cattlemen of Texas*, was his early association with the

Texas Cattle Raisers' Association: "Mr. Blocker became affiliated with the Texas Cattle Raisers' Association soon after its organization, and as a member, has worked for all important improvements in the industry that have been attained during the last two decades [1890–1910]" (65). The association was founded with the stated purpose to "systematize the 'spring work' and to curb cattle rustling" (Marshall et. al., 6:417–418). One of the methods for combating cattle rustling that was initiated by the Texas and Southwestern Cattle Raisers Association (as it became) was the development of its own law enforcement body devoted to investigating and prosecuting cattle theft. These were the Special Rangers who were paid by the association but were commissioned by the State of Texas:

> The association originally hired investigators who served as deputies in each county they worked. In the early 1900s, though, the men were told they couldn't serve two masters and were commissioned as "Special Rangers," giving them jurisdiction over several counties. Although they are deputized, the inspectors are employed by the association, not the State of Texas.
>
> (JACOBS B-1)

Alfred Y. Allee, according to his grandson, had been appointed a Special Ranger, but the Texas State Archives, the depository for the Ranger appointments, has no record of this. Perhaps the incident with Brack Cornett, the bank and train robber killed by Allee, provided the basis for the claim made by Allee's descendants that "Grandpa Allee" had become a Special Ranger. In that instance, though, the employing agency may have been the express company that paid the $3,800 reward to Allee after he killed Cornett, rather than the Cattle Raisers.

Returning to Alonzo Allee, we can imagine that the ten days he spent in the Webb County jail before his lawyer bailed him out filled him with anxiety, in spite of his familiarity with the judicial process. After all, J. B. Compton had been hanged within the confines of the same jail only five months earlier. Calmer reflection, though, would have assuaged that anxiety. Unlike Compton and his accomplice, who had been unable to hire legal counsel and had court-appointed lawyers, Alonzo Allee had three lawyers working on his behalf whose fees did not come from the tax coffers.

Allee was also on friendly terms with the local lawmen, such as

Deputy Sheriffs J. E. Hill and Sam McKenzie. Deputy Sheriff McKenzie, one of the two deputies (along with Willie Stoner) who first reached the scene of the crime, may have been one and the same as Sam McKenzie, a Texas Ranger who would frequent the ranch where Alonzo Allee and his family lived at some unspecified time. A. Y. Allee, Alonzo's son, reminisced:

> All during this time [while A. Y. was growing up] my father also worked as a Special Ranger. . . . Back in those days, they didn't have much money to pay Rangers, so they appointed Special Rangers which were called on when they were needed. I got to know many of the old regular Rangers . . . Will Wright, Cleave Hearst, *Sam Mckenzie* [emphasis added] . . . men like that. They would stop by and camp a few days at the ranch. . . . We always had a bunch of ol' Spanish goats, so we would have *cabrito*, and I always was interested in their stories.   (PATTIE, "A. Y." 43)

There is no evidence that Alonzo Allee was a Special Ranger in 1912. However, Allee must have felt that he was among friends, even if he was in jail, and prosecution for the killing of the Gutiérrez men may have seemed a remote possibility, especially after he was released on bail in late August. If he thought about the Compton execution, it would have been to note the speedy turning of the wheels of justice in that case, unlike in his own situation. In the Compton-Franks case, Thompson tells us:

> Two days later [after the arrest], in a rare example of judicial expediency, Compton and Franks were indicted for first degree murder by a hastily called grand jury consisting of some of the more prominent and influential citizens in Webb County, including L. R. Ortiz, P. P. Leyendecker, A. Bertani, Eugene Christen and A. M. Bruni.   (254)

It was not until late October, some two months after Allee's release from jail on bond, that District Judge John F. Mullally convened the grand jury to consider, among other matters scheduled for the court's regular calendar, the case against Alonzo W. Allee for the killings of Francisco and Manuel Gutiérrez.

On October 29, 1912, the *Laredo Daily Times* reported:

The November term of the district court of the 49th judicial district for Webb County will be convened by Judge J. F. Mullally. It is probable that a number of important cases on the docket will come up for trial, including the case against Alonzo Allee, charged with the killing in this county several months ago of Francisco and Manuel Gutierrez.

The grand jury will be chosen from the following: Eugene Christen, Joe Leyendecker, Joe Henry, J. E. Biggio, Amador Garcia, B. W. Masterson, J. A. Rodriguez, J. C. Martin, W. N. Young, Tom Attlee, A. Bertani, B. A. Puig, John Convery, Leopoldo Villegas, Antonio Salinas and J. E. Hill.

The grand jury panel being composed, as Thompson says, of the prominent citizens of the county, it is not surprising that some of the same names appear here as did in the Compton case. And since public officials were considered, ipso facto, prominent citizens, it should not surprise us either that certain members of the panel were indeed public officials. The photographs and names of these officials appear in Falvella's *Souvenir Album*, for example, Eugene Christen, the fire marshal of the City of Laredo and brother of L. J. Christen, the city superintendent of schools; J. A. Rodríguez, Webb County clerk; and J. C. Martin, city tax assessor. J. E. Hill we have already met as the deputy sheriff who escorted Alonzo Allee to jail.

From this panel twelve were selected, according to the *Laredo Daily Times* of November 6. They were: "L. Villegas, foreman; Christen, Biggio, Young, Leyendecker, Garcia, Henry, Martin, Bertani, Hill, Salinas, Rodriguez."

In 1916, according to Falvella, Laredo had a population of more than 25,000 (*Album* 18). Falvella may have been optimistic or engaging in boosterism. The census of 1910 gave the population of Webb County as 22,503. However, undercounting is a common failing of census numbers, and we must remember that between 1910 and 1916 Webb County had seen a significant influx of population—refugees fleeing from the Mexican Revolution.

If in 1900 Anglos represented one-fourth of the population of Webb County, as stated in the *New Handbook of Texas* (6:865), it is most probable that the ratio remained unchanged or at most increased slightly by 1912. (Beginning in 1913, though, the Mexican population increased in South Texas as revolutionary violence gained momentum in Mexico.) It is remarkable, then, that so few Spanish surnames—only four out of twelve, or a third of the grand jury—appear in this body. If 75 percent of the population of Webb County was Mexican or of Mexican origin, the composition of the grand jury could be expected to reflect, or at least approximate, this demographic profile. But that would mean looking at the situation after more than fifty years of legislation and litigation over civil rights have transpired, with today's sensibilities rather than those of 1912.

Actually, in the Laredo of 1912, the fact that a person carried an Anglo surname did not automatically make that person Anglo from either an ethnic or a cultural standpoint. The ancestry of some of the non-Spanish-surnamed individuals could be traced back to marriages between Anglos and descendants of the original settlers of Laredo, the Creole-Spaniards. An example of such an intermarriage was that of Hamilton P. Bee, the Confederate general, who first arrived in Laredo as a young officer accompanying Mirabeau B. Lamar during the Mexican War. Bee made Laredo his home and went on to become the first county clerk of Webb County in 1849. According to Thompson, Bee married Andrea Martínez of Laredo, and their daughter, Lamar, married Cristóbal Benavides, of the prominent Benavides family of Laredo, in 1867 (158).

Others with non-Spanish surnames were descendants of Europeans who settled in Laredo before the signing of the Treaty of Guadalupe Hidalgo in 1848. At that time Laredo was still officially part of Mexico, although occupied by American troops, and wanted to remain part of Mexico, as the petition in early 1848 from the Laredo City Council (*ayuntamiento*) to the governments of both Mexico and the United States requested (Hinojosa 58). One of the Europeans who settled in occupied Laredo was John Z. Leyendecker, a German who arrived in Laredo in 1847 and married Andrea Benavides in 1857. After Andrea's death, Leyendecker married her sister, Juliana, with whom he had ten children (Thompson 115). It was a descendant of John Z. Leyendecker, Joe Leyendecker, who sat on the grand jury during the November 1912 term of the Forty-ninth District Court.

There was also on that grand jury of November 1912 at least one first-generation European immigrant, Andrés (or Andrea) Bertani, who was born in the region of Parma, in Italy, in 1851. Bertani emigrated to the United States in 1872, locating first in San Antonio, where he clerked for various mercantile firms. In 1881 Bertani moved to Laredo and established a small retail store. Bertani's biography appeared in *Twentieth*

Century History of Southwest Texas, which was published in 1907 and contained a chapter on Laredo. According to the anonymous biographer, Bertani's business in Laredo grew and prospered until "he built a large establishment, wholesale and retail, handling dry goods, groceries, clothing, hardware implements and general supplies for both the city and ranch trade" (115).

In the "Inventory and List of Claims of the Estate of Manuel Gutiérrez, Deceased," which was filed on October 9, 1912, with the probate court and is found in the Webb County Probate Records, the following debts, incurred by the deceased shortly before his death, were listed:

> One promissory note for the sum of $2,280 Dollars dated
> May 26th 1911, with interest at the rate of $ [*sic*] 10 per cent
> per annum from date, payable to the order of A. Bertani . . . said
> note is secured by mortgage on cattle. Note due 4 months after
> its date. Another note for $5,760, dated Feby 27th 1912, due
> 5 years after date; interest from its date at—% per annum
> due A. Bertani secured by mortgage on land. And open account
> due A. Bertani for $228.00.

From a small retail merchant, Andrea Bertani had expanded to moneylender to the area ranchers, as well as supplying their everyday needs on credit. If anyone perceived a conflict of interest in Bertani sitting on the grand jury inquiring into the death of a man who had owed him a substantial amount of money, that person kept his doubts to himself. But, most likely, the question never arose.

The foreman of the grand jury, Leopoldo Villegas, was the most prominent Spanish-surnamed member of that body, but he was not, as might be expected, descended from the founding families of Laredo. Like another prominent Laredoan involved in this case—John Anthony Valls, the district attorney—Leopoldo Villegas was the son of a Spanish immigrant who had settled in the border area in the second half of the nineteenth century. Leopoldo Villegas was the son of Don Joaquín Villegas, who was born in the province of Santander in northern Spain. It may be fanciful to imagine that Don Joaquín had decided to settle in Laredo—or, more precisely, in Nuevo Laredo—because its name, if not its geography, reminded him of home. In any case, this flight of fancy might be better attributed to Don José de Escandón, who gave the name of a fishing village on the Bay of Biscay—Laredo—to his settlement of San

Agustín de Laredo (now Laredo, Texas), on the banks of the Rio Grande and located in the province of Nuevo Santander.

Don Joaquín Villegas, together with his brother, Quintín, established a commercial firm in Nuevo Laredo and from there conducted a wholesale trade on both sides of the border. By 1907, when *Twentieth Century History of Southwest Texas* was published, the two brothers had retired from the business, passing its management to the younger generation who carried on under the name of L. Villegas & Bro. The "L." could have referred to either of Don Joaquín's sons, Leopoldo or Lorenzo, since they had the same initial (83–84).

Leopoldo and Lorenzo were not the only Villegas children who held a prominent position in Laredo. Their sister, Leonor, who after her marriage was known as Leonor Villegas de Magnón, became, along with Jovita Idar, one of the early feminist leaders of Laredo and was a frequent contributor to *La Crónica,* Nicasio Idar's newspaper. Leonor's activities during the Mexican Revolution and her writings, which were later published as *La Rebelde,* merited her an entry in the *New Handbook of Texas* (6:753–754). After the Villegas family moved from Nuevo Laredo to Laredo, Texas, following the outbreak of the Mexican Revolution, Leonor also organized a Mexican civic club called Sociedad, Unión, Progreso y Caridad (Society, Unity, Progress and Charity) with the purpose of improving the situation of the poorer Mexicans. The activities of this club were frequently publicized in the pages of the *Laredo Daily Times,* although this newspaper normally covered mostly Anglo-American activities (Hinojosa 119).

The author of the chapter on Laredo and its prominent citizens that appeared in *A Twentieth Century History of Southwest Texas* concluded the section on the Villegas family by saying the following about the firm L. Villegas & Bro.: "They are following the business methods of their predecessors, and it is needless to state that they are successful therein. The firm is one of the largest on the border and does an exclusive wholesale and commission business, also imports and exports" (84).

High praise indeed in 1907, not only for the Villegas family, but for Laredo itself as an unusually integrated community. The author shows a remarkable degree of open-mindedness, which he demonstrates by quoting from an article by E. R. Tarver in the *San Antonio Express.* This was the same E. R. Tarver whose 1889 pamphlet for the Laredo Immigration Society had touted Laredo to the rest of the country, so perhaps a grain of salt is called for in reading this paean. On the other hand,

Tarver knew well the area about which he wrote. The 1900 *General Directory of the City of Laredo* lists him as state representative for the 86th District, as well as Webb County superintendent of public instruction (11). Tarver wrote:

> The population of the City [Laredo] has grown from 5,000 to over 15,000 in 1907. When the railroads reached here 95 per cent of the people were Mexicans. Today about 75 per cent are of the same nationality.
>
> Though politics has become warm and exciting at times since the advent of the Americans and though they only poll 25 per cent of the vote, yet the Mexican people have been generous enough to divide the county and city offices with them all the time.
>
> Notwithstanding these facts, you often hear Americans saying that these Mexicans should not be allowed to vote.
>
> *(Twentieth Century History 76)*

There seems to have been a serpent in Tarver's paradise. The Anglo minority, in spite of commanding a far greater proportion of influence and political power than its numbers would seem to have warranted, appeared to be chafing at having to share any power at all. Indeed, it seems that the goal of the Anglos who arrived in Webb County in the late 1870s and early 1880s was to dominate local government, and they had succeeded in doing so by the turn of the century. The historian Roberto R. Calderón describes this development: "In the course of the 1880s . . . the Anglo minority, its numbers bolstered by increased migration, succeeded in electing majorities in both the city and county governments" (675–676). Calderón agrees with Tarver's view of the generosity of the Mexican people, adding: "The majority Mexican electorate acquiesced in making possible the new electoral norm" (676). But apparently the Mexican generosity—or acquiescence—did not elicit reciprocal feelings of tolerance from the Anglo minority. The unfolding of the Gutiérrez case would show the degree to which hostility and resentfulness prevailed among the latecomer Anglos.

After the grand jury was seated on November 6, 1912, it took them only two days—until November 8—to issue indictments charging Alonzo W.

Allee with murder in the killings of Francisco and Manuel Gutiérrez. The first indictment, signed by L. Villegas, foreman, read:

> The Grand Jurors for the County of Webb, State aforesaid [Texas], duly organized as such, at the November term, a.d. 1912 of the District Court for said County upon their oaths in said Court, present that Alonzo W. Allee in the County and State aforesaid on or about the 14th day of August A.D. 1912 did then and there with malice aforethought kill Francisco Gutierrez Garza by shooting him with a gun.

The second indictment recited the same charge, except that it pertained to the killing of Manuel Gutiérrez García.

Bond was immediately set for Allee at $15,000 in each case, but the amount posed no problem for the defendant. Sureties were standing by. The *Laredo Daily Times* reported on November 9 that the $30,000 bond had been posted by W. W. Jones, R. L. Henrichsen, Covey C. Thomas, and F. Vandervoort. This last individual was a member of the prominent Vandervoort family of Carrizo Springs that included one of Allee's attorneys, J. Vandervoort.

The prompt return of the two indictments says something about the effective management of the grand jury business by its foreman. However, it may also be indicative of the strength of the evidence that was presented to this body. That evidence would have consisted primarily of the testimony taken at the inquest conducted by the coroner, Nicasio Idar, the day after the killings.

The sparse case records contain only the statements of three witnesses and Idar's own notes of his observations at the scene of the crime. The latter described the condition of the victims, as Idar found them, and the place where the events occurred. However, we must remember that the crime scene had remained unsecured for hours before the authorities arrived. We do not know what, if anything, Allee had done between the time that he shot his victims and when he fled from La Volanta. We do not know, therefore, if the scene that Idar found and described had remained undisturbed after the shootings.

The witnesses who gave their testimony to Justice of the Peace Nicasio Idar were Laureano and Francisco Gutiérrez García, brothers, children of Julián Gutiérrez and nephews of Don Francisco Gutiérrez Garza. The third witness was Julián Gutiérrez, their father. It can be safely assumed that none of them spoke English and that they gave their testimony in Spanish. The testimony was then taken down in writing— but in English.

As a public official, Nicasio Idar would have been expected to know English. However, his transcription of the witnesses' testimony reveals that English was not his first language. His syntax, and particularly his spelling, are often erratic, and only by referring to Spanish can some of the phraseology be understood. Before we judge Idar's linguistic shortcomings too harshly, though, we must bear in mind that conducting the interview in Spanish while transcribing it into English almost simultaneously was no easy feat.

The statements of these three witnesses are the only contemporaneous sources that we have for the events that took place at La Volanta Ranch on August 14, 1912. For this reason it is imperative to present the testimony in its entirety:

> Laureano Gutiérrez, after being duly sworn, says:
> I live with father in Cantarito Ranch about one mile from La Volanta Ranch. I am a cowboy. I was employed by Lonnie Allee to work for him as cowboy on Augt. 14th 1912 and about eleven a.m. while I was preparing dinner for Mr. Allee and four other persons, I heard a quarrell between Mr. Allee and Manuel Gutiérrez García and Francisco Gutiérrez Garza. I came to see what was the trouble and they quit quarreling and set down. I went back to my work and then I heard the steps of Mr. Allee, and I came to see what it was. And I saw Mr. Allee go to where his coat was hanging and took his pistol therefrom, and came back with the pistol in his hand and said to them: I am as good a man as any Mexican. My uncle Francisco told him to put away his pistol, that it was not a question of fight. And he, Lonnie, immeadiately fired a shot at Manuel [and he] fell and I ran out of the room and got on my horse and went to the heard and told my brother that Allee had shot Manuel, and for us to go, and notify Rosendo and the family at the Ranch Las Mujeres.
> While they were quareling I heard Francisco Gutiérrez Garza ask Allee to sign a contract. This were the last words I heard before the shooting.

> It was signed "Laureano Gutiérrez."

Laureano's most damning testimony was his description of how Allee had walked to where his coat was hanging, taken his pistol from a pocket, while both Gutiérrez men, who had been sitting down, tried to reason with him as he shot them. Nicasio Idar translated Don Francisco's response as an admonishment to Allee to put away his pistol, telling him that it was not "a question of fight." Oral family history passed down the actual words, which were in Spanish, as "Esto no es cosa de armas" ("This is not a matter for weapons"). Those were Don Francisco's last words.

It was not a matter for weapons in Don Francisco and Manuel's way of looking at things. But it was for Alonzo W. Allee. It was particularly a matter for weapons if Allee felt that he was "as good a man as any Mexican" and if he felt that he had been treated as less than was his rightful due.

Laureano, unarmed, ran from the room where Allee had just shot Manuel Gutiérrez and left the ranch house to go get help. He rode his horse to where his brother was with "the heard." Nicasio Idar clearly misspelled "herd," as in "herd of cattle." The word is easily misspelled, even by native speakers of English, and English, as we have said, was not Idar's primary language. Neither was ranching. Each occupation or field of activity has its own vocabulary. Nicasio Idar was a journalist. With other members of his family, he published *La Crónica* and other Spanish-language newspapers. In translating Laureano Gutiérrez's words, he had to do so, not only from Spanish to English, but also from Spanish ranching terms to their equivalent in English. Someone familiar with ranching activities would perhaps say, in English, that he had gone to where his brother was "with the cattle," or "working cattle." Nonetheless, we get the gist that Laureano's brother was some distance away (since Laureano had to ride his horse to get to him), occupied with the cattle.

Laureano's purpose in telling his brother was to get help, not only from him, but also from their nearest neighbors, "Rosendo and the family at the Ranch of Las Mujeres." "Rosendo" was Rosendo Rodríguez, another Mexican rancher in northeast Webb County whose land adjoined the Gutiérrez land to the east. In one instance, a narrow strip of land, section 1525, patented to Víctor Rodríguez, separated two of Don Francisco's sections, 480 and 1030. A stream, known as Las Mujeres Creek, traversed section 1029, also patented to Víctor Rodríguez, and gave the ranch its name. This section lies due east of Don Francisco's section 1030 on the Webb County land map.

The words that had precipitated the shooting had been Don Francisco's, insisting that Allee "sign a contract," according to Laureano. That insistence had prompted Allee to retort that he was "as good a man as any Mexican." We can only speculate as to whether Allee truly felt affronted by the demand, which was no more than ordinary business practice, or if there was a more nefarious reason for his refusal to sign the lease. Did Allee's reply indicate that he felt singled out, that he was being treated with less consideration than a Mexican would receive? Did he feel that he was the victim of a double standard—that Mexicans did business among themselves based on the proverbial handshake while they insisted on written documents from Anglos? There is a flavor of resentment, as well as arrogance, in those words uttered by Allee before he pulled the trigger. The resentment and arrogance were fused into anger at being placed in a subordinate position—that of a tenant to his Mexican landlord—and also call to mind those Anglos mentioned by Tarver who resented having Mexicans in political office, or even voting.

The next witness whose statement was transcribed by Nicasio Idar was Francisco Gutiérrez García, Laureano's brother. Francisco's testimony was, of course, limited to what his brother had told him and was, therefore, brief:

> Francisco Gutiérrez García after being duly sworn says:
> I am employed by Lonnie Allee. I live at the Cantarito ranch about a mile from the place where the shutting occurred. I was at heard on the 14th of this month August 1912 when my brother Laureano came and told me that: my brother Manuel and my uncle Francisco have just been killed. [Signed: Francisco Gutiérrez.]

Strictly speaking, Laureano only knew about Manuel being shot, so that when he told his brother that his uncle Francisco had also been killed, Laureano was not accurate. However, he probably felt that Don Francisco's death was a foregone conclusion, and he was right. The only confusion in the text, apart from "shutting" for "shooting" and the reference to being "at heard," is the reference to Manuel Gutiérrez as "my brother." This is easily explained by pointing out that in Spanish first cousins, such as Francisco and Manuel were, are *primos hermanos*. A first cousin was often referred to in those days simply as an *hermano* (brother), rather than a *primo*. The usage reflected not only a lexical shorthand but also a closer feeling of kinship among the extended family than is prevalent today. As a footnote, we can also comment here on the use of the surnames of both parents among the Spanish and Spanish-Americans. This practice serves the very useful purpose of differentiating persons with the same given name and paternal surname. Thus, Nicasio Idar properly and accurately identifies and differentiates Francisco Gutiérrez García, the son of Julián Gutiérrez and Catarina García, from his uncle, the deceased Francisco Gutiérrez Garza.

Julián Gutiérrez also appears in Nicasio Idar's report, giving brief testimony as to the reason for his brother's presence at La Volanta and his visit to Allee:

> Julián Gutiérrez being duly sworn says:
> My name is as above. I live in my ranch: Los Cantaritos. My brother Francisco Gutiérrez lived in Guerrero, Tamaulipas, Mexico, and on the 2d instant he told me that he had come to have Mr. Allee [sign] some papers about the land of la Bolanta. Julián Gutiérrez "X" his mark.

This short testimony gives, nonetheless, additional information. It tells us that Don Francisco had been either in Laredo or at Los Cantaritos (most likely Laredo, where Julián also had a home) since at least August 2. This strengthens the hypothesis that Don Francisco, having come for an extended visit to Laredo, was probably accompanied by his wife and that while there he attended to the legal business of the new lease for La Volanta, and also visited with his son and his daughter, as well as his brother. From Julián's testimony we can also infer that the communication between the two brothers about La Volanta had been oral and not by letter—indicating a personal visit. Julián's statement bears an "X" mark at the end, instead of a signature. The most obvious inference from this observation is that Julián could not sign his name because he was illiterate, and, indeed, in the 1910 census of Webb County Julián Gutiérrez had indicated that he could neither read nor write.

For anyone who has the opportunity of seeing the beautifully precise signature of Francisco Gutiérrez Garza, as it appears in documents found in the Municipal Archives of Nueva Ciudad Guerrero, Tamaulipas, Mexico, it is difficult to imagine that his brother could be illiterate. However, Francisco was born in 1842, Julián in 1850. In the middle of the nineteenth century Mexico was racked by wars and uprisings, not least among which were the Texas Rebellion (as it was called there) and the war with the United States that cost Mexico a great part of its territory. Schooling in the small towns along the Rio Grande at that time was sporadic and subject to many interruptions by the invasions and rebellions. Under those conditions, educating children was, perforce, rationed; not all got to go to school.

Another fact of life in those days and in that agrarian society was the widely-held opinion that not all children needed to be educated in book learning. If a child—a boy—showed greater inclination toward physical activity than toward more refined pursuits, he would be promptly "destined for the ranch" by the family. In that instance, learning the numbers and basic arithmetic might be the extent of his training, although by the nature of his work he also acquired vast knowledge in the properties and characteristics of plants and animals, rudimentary veterinary medicine, astronomy and climatology. Thus, it would not have been unusual for José Manuel Gutiérrez and María Antonia de la Garza, the parents of Francisco and Julián, to have Francisco, the eldest child, learn to read and write "a beautiful hand" while Julián, the second son and third child (out of six), would have been put to doing ranch work.

Further analysis of the text of Julián's statement tells us little else about Julián or the events in question, but it reveals something of Nicasio Idar's state of mind in transcribing the testimony. That Idar must have been harried, distracted and even, perhaps, distraught can be adduced from the omission of the verb "signed" from the sentence ending in "he told me that he had come to have Mr. Allee—some papers about the land of la Bolanta." In the spelling of the name of the ranch Idar deviates from the usual *Volanta.* However, since Spanish makes little distinction between the pronunciation of "b" and "v," the spelling of words containing either letter tended to be somewhat fluid, and even nowadays the confusion still occurs, although less frequently with proper names.

One additional comment on all three statements is called for, and it pertains to the manner in which the three Gutiérrez men—Julián and his two sons—refer to Alonzo Allee. Laureano and Francisco both make reference to being employed by "Lonnie Allee." Julián, though, refers to him as Mr. Allee. This may seem odd at first blush, in light of the fact that Julián Gutiérrez was sixty-two and Alonzo Allee was thirty-four. However, the title *Señor Allee,* as it would have been used by Julián, would have denoted distance, in the sense of lack of familiarity, rather than deference. In other words, Alonzo Allee was a stranger as far as Julián Gutiérrez was concerned. On the other hand, to Laureano, who was twenty-five, and Francisco, who was nineteen, Alonzo Allee was "Lonnie," as to friends and acquaintances. Both boys were relatively close in age to Allee, which may have been the reason for the familiarity, but, on the other hand, they could have been acquiescing to Allee's wish to be called by his nickname, a reflection of the "flatter social hierarchy in the United States," as Tracy Novinger terms it in *Intercultural Communication: A Practical Guide* (137).

Likewise, Laureano and Francisco would have addressed "Lonnie" with the familiar *tú,* whereas their father and their uncle would have used the formal *usted,* not, as we said before, out of deference but as a way of keeping their distance. "Mr. Allee" reflects distance and perhaps—but not always—respect. To show respect, coupled with warmth, the Gutiérrez men, like all other Mexicans, would have used the honorific "Don," followed by the man's first name, as in "Don Francisco."

One final note on the witnesses' testimony: Laureano states that he was preparing dinner for his employer "and four other persons." There is no evidence that anyone else was present in the ranch house, besides the four already mentioned—Allee, Laureano, Don Francisco and Manuel Gutiérrez. Perhaps Idar misunderstood Laureano as he translated the testimony, or the guests had not yet arrived when the killings occurred.

The second part of Nicasio Idar's report on the killings contains his notes on the state of the bodies and a description of the scene of the crime, as he found it. In those days law enforcement agencies, especially in rural areas, did not have the full panoply of "scene of the crime" equipment and experts, as they have today. The Webb County sheriff's office did not even use a photographer to photograph the bodies or their surroundings in this case. It fell to the coroner, Idar, to not only interview the witnesses, but also to draw sketches of the victims, as he did in a rudimentary fashion. From this investigation the coroner made the determination as to the cause of death and as to whether the deaths were the result of a crime, as he was required to do by law.

The duties and powers of the coroner under Texas law were described as follows in the case of *Pierson v. Galveston County* (Civ. App. 1939) 131 S.W.2d 27:

> Generally, the purpose of a "coroner's inquest" is to obtain information as to whether a death was caused by some criminal act and to obtain evidence to prevent escape of the guilty, as well as to furnish a foundation for criminal prosecution in case the death is shown to be felonious.

Nicasio Idar's investigation into the Gutiérrez killings shows him to have diligently discharged his statutory duty, but his was only the first step in the judicial process. Once Idar's part was over, the matter was out of his hands. But in the meantime he furnished the prosecution with a graphic description of what he saw at La Volanta.

Nicasio Idar drew two crude outlines intended to represent the body of Manuel Gutiérrez from the front and the back, pointing to the places where the bullet wounds were located and appended a written description of the drawings.

> Manuel Gutiérrez García had his pistol in his hand and his finger in the trigger. One catdridge snapped—
>
> I examined the empty shell and appeared to have been recently fired—
>
> There was the mark of a shot fired at feet of Manuel—

The outline on the left of the page shows a view of Manuel's body from the back. A dot in the middle of the back, about two-thirds of the way between the shoulders and the waist, has the caption: "One shot in the back." Another dot, higher up and toward the reader's right (the body's left), approximately where a lung would be, is captioned: "No 1 came out the shoulder blade—on left side."

The second figure, labeled "front," has a dot with a line pointing to it and a caption: "No 1 front shot/ 3 inches above the left nipple."

Below the two outlines of a man's body (Manuel) is the drawing of a square with a dot midway along the vertical left side. The caption reads: "Middle door" and "One shot at the door here [the dot]." Then, "Front door two shots through it."

At the bottom of the page Idar begins the description of Don Francisco's body:

The old man was shot over the heart. He had his pistol in the scabert.

Francisco Gutiérrez Garza had his pistol in his scabt with 4 catridges, neither one of them was fired—and the pistol was in the scabet

One shot right in the heart and came out in the right shoulder.

There is no drawing to accompany this description, and so we are left not knowing if the shot through the heart that killed Don Francisco truly came out the right shoulder, indicating perhaps a diagonal trajectory, or if Idar made a mistake and should have written "left" shoulder, instead.

We should also clarify Idar's use of the terms "scabert, scabt, scabet." They are obviously misspellings of "scabbard," defined by Funk & Wagnell's Dictionary as "a sheath for a weapon, as for a bayonet or a sword." In other words, Francisco Gutiérrez Garza still had his pistol in the holster when he was shot through the heart.

Manuel had apparently tried to defend himself and managed to fire one shot, but he never had a chance against a man who had had his pistol already in his hand before Manuel began to draw and who fired first. Manuel's shot clearly did not hit Allee. It was probably the one that landed at Manuel's feet, the shot fired by a man already mortally wounded. If, indeed, Manuel fired at all. Laureano had fled after the first shot, and we do not know what Allee did when he was left alone with the two dead men. It is not unheard of to put a gun in a dead person's hand and squeeze the trigger with the lifeless finger, thus laying the foundation for a claim of self-defense.

The other six shots—two into Manuel, one into Don Francisco, one shot through the middle door and two through the front door—came from Allee's fully loaded .45 caliber revolver. He had emptied his gun inside the room. It was fortunate for young Laureano Gutiérrez that he had quick reflexes; otherwise, there would have been three dead men, instead of two.

This double tragedy leaves the reader figuratively wringing his or her hands, wondering if there was any way that it could have been avoided. The situation at La Volanta on August 14, 1912, brings to mind a remark from a popular movie of the 1960s, *Cool Hand Luke* (1967), in which the hero, the leader in a prison uprising, remarks, albeit ironically, to his antagonist, the prison warden, "What we have here is a failure to communicate." That summer day at La Volanta there was certainly a failure in the mode of communication. Don Francisco Gutiérrez communicated with a legal document; Alonzo W. Allee used a gun.

Alonzo Allee responded to the demand that he sign a lease if he wanted to remain at La Volanta by drawing his gun. This response took father and son by surprise. Decent people were not supposed to behave like that. Even in view of Allee's action, Don Francisco did not draw his own weapon in self-defense. Instead, he remonstrated with Allee, telling him that their discussion was "not a matter for weapons," almost as if he were giving Allee a lesson in civility—or etiquette.

Don Francisco and his son were both armed, but it was more as a precaution. Men carried weapons then as a matter of course, especially in the country, where coyotes, rattlesnakes and bobcats posed a danger, as well as the occasional "desperado." But people like Don Francisco and Manuel did not engage in a gunfight within the four walls of their own house, not even when provoked by a troublesome tenant. They were *gente decente* or *gente de bien*. But Alonzo Allee was not.

These terms, *gente decente* and *gente de bien*, meaning the "good, decent, respectable people," came to be abbreviated as *gente bien* while suffering a depreciation in value during recent times. *Gente bien* came to connote pretentiousness and smugness, and people so described became objects of ridicule, as in *Las niñas bien*, the ironically titled book by the contemporary Mexican author Guadalupe Loaeza. In one of her unflattering portraits of the *gente bien*, Loaeza writes: "Intentaré pues . . . hacer una radiografía rápida de esa 'gente bien,' es decir, la 'gente decente,' la GCU, 'gente como uno.'" ("I will try, then, . . . to take a quick X-ray of the 'good people,' that is, the 'decent people,' the 'people like oneself'" [60]).

Loaeza's critical attitude about the "good people" can be traced back to Mariano Azuela's novels of the Mexican Revolution, in particular *Las tribulaciones de una familia decente (The Tribulations of a Decent Family)*, which describes the harsh effects of the Revolution on an upper-class family of hacendados. The term *decente*, as used by Azuela in the title of his novel, is meant to be ironic. John Rutherford, in his book, *Mexican Society during the Revolution: A Literary Approach*, elucidates on the etymology of the term *gente decente* in Azuela and other writers:

It is worth referring, in passing, to the class overtones of the word "decente," as it is used in the title of this novel [Azuela's]. By the nineteenth century this adjective had undergone interesting semantic change, and both in Spain and Spanish America it had come to mean not only "decent" but also aristocratic (clearly because of the conviction that ruling classes normally have that they alone are honorable and respectable—indeed the latter word has in English acquired comparable, though less marked, class significance.) Many of the novelists of the Revolution use the word with its second meaning (which became quite independent of its original moral sense), but none more than Azuela, who constantly exploited the ironic possibilities of this linguistic situation. The most notable example (among dozens) is a scene in *Los de abajo* [*The Underdogs*] where a woman begs money from the revolutionary soldiery, claiming that her suitcase has been stolen: "Gentlemen, a *señor decente* stole my suitcase at Silao station." (246–247)

However, in even more recent times, among scholars in the United States, the term *gente decente* has begun to be vindicated, shedding its ironic overtones, and being used in the way that Mexican-Americans and Mexicans of the border area would have used it in the early twentieth-century. Leticia Garza-Falcón, for example, titled her study of Mexican-American literature *Gente Decente: A Borderlands Response to the Rhetoric of Dominance.* In her book Garza-Falcón studies the works of several Mexican-American writers, some contemporary, some from the early part of the twentieth century, who portray Mexican characters that refute the negative Mexican stereotypes found in American—particularly Texan—history and popular culture, such as novels and movies. Of one such writer, Jovita González, Garza-Falcón says:

> . . . For our own times, the story of the representative struggle of Jovita González between her identity as a South Texas Mexicana of limited financial means, with a strict *gente decente* consciousness, and that of a scholar wanting to fit within the Anglo academic world encircling the University of Texas during the 1920s and 1930s is most valuable. (10)

Another writer, Elliot Young, studied the *gente decente* of Laredo in his article, "Deconstructing *La Raza:* Identifying the *Gente Decente* of Laredo, 1904 to 1911." Young explains the purpose of his article by stating that it "explores the struggles over the definitions of racial, class and gender identities which occurred in Laredo's Mexican community at the beginning of the twentieth century" (228). However, Young goes on to define the *gente decente* of Laredo in a manner that denies the fluidity of the border and the existence of transnational families that we have noted before: "During the first decade of this century [twentieth], the Mexican elites of Laredo attempted to distinguish themselves from other Mexicans migrating to Texas by highlighting their own respectability, high level of education and honorable culture. I refer to this group as the *gente decente* . . ." (228).

Under Young's definition Manuel Gutiérrez would have been seen in Laredo as part of the rabble because he had recently moved from Ciudad Guerrero, Tamaulipas, to Laredo, Texas. Not even the newspapers reporting his death made that mistake. Young is correct, though, in pointing out that inclusion among the *gente decente* did not depend on economic status: "Belonging to the *gente decente* depended upon one's education, comportment, family background and participation in Laredo's civic societies" (229).

Comportment, which in Spanish is part of *educación,* or education, but is much more than formal schooling, was certainly the key to being or not being *gente decente.* Among the *gente decente* one did not settle one's differences with a volley of gunfire. That was left to thugs and bandits. But among Alonzo Allee's group—and certainly his family—they did, not necessarily because they were uncouth—which they may have been—but because they had found that violence and intimidation were very effective means of achieving domination.

On that August day of 1912 at La Volanta there was certainly a breakdown in communication, but not because Alonzo Allee ignored good manners. Allee had learned at his father's knee that the gun settled questions quickly and with finality. There was no need for manners, good or otherwise.

Part III

SO GREAT A PREJUDICE

A scant three days before the grand jury handed down the two indictments charging Alonzo Allee with the murders of Francisco and Manuel Gutiérrez, Webb County, along with the rest of the country, voted in the general election of 1912. On Wednesday, November 6, 1912, the *Laredo Daily Times* reported that "Texas gave [Woodrow] Wilson the greatest vote ever cast for president" and that "Taft and [Theodore] Roosevelt combined received less votes than cast for Taft in 1908." In this election Laredo and Webb County proved that E. R. Tarver, in saying that the Mexican people in Laredo had "been generous enough to divide the county and city offices with them [the Anglo-Americans]," had not known the full extent of this generosity. Webb County not only divided its public offices between Anglos and Mexicans. It also divided them between Democrats and Republicans.

On the Democratic side of the local ballot, November 5, 1912, saw the reelection of Sheriff Amador Sánchez and County Attorney Juan V. Benavides, while the *Laredo Daily Times* of November 6 reported: MULLALLY AND VALLS RECEIVED A LARGE MAJORITY OVER DEMOCRATIC NOMINEES FOR THE OFFICE. It was clear that the Webb County voters did not vote a straight ticket. The reelection of both District Judge John F. Mullally and District Attorney John A. Valls to their respective offices on the Forty-ninth Judicial District was all the more remarkable because they not only outpolled their Democratic opponents, but they outpolled their fellow Republicans, as well. The *Daily Times* reported on November 6, 1912, that "the heavy vote for the Republican candidates for district judge and district attorney, however, was no criterion of how the county went, as the Republican ticket otherwise triumphed by a majority of only about 400 votes, while Mullally and Valls carried Webb County by about 900 majority."

The newspaper had reported earlier that voter turnout in Webb County had been heavy for the general election, "the total [vote] approximating 1,578." Out of those 1,578 votes, Mullally and Valls had each polled 1,098 votes, or about 70 percent of the total. A few days later, the *Laredo Weekly Times* of November 10, 1912 (the Sunday edition), updated the vote numbers: "With Ward 3 still to report, the vote was Mullally 1698 to Hudson 277 and Valls 1698 to Phelps 277."

In the minds of the voters of Webb County, Mullally and Valls were, literally, a team, and the long association of the two men bore out this view. In *The Kingdom of Zapata,* Lott and Martínez quote Seb Wilcox, the long-time court reporter of the Forty-ninth District Court, who knew both Mullally and Valls:

> The Forty-ninth Judicial District, composed of Webb, Duval and Zapata counties, was created and organized in 1891. Judge A. L. McLane of Laredo was appointed district judge, and Honorable Marshall Hicks of Laredo was named as district attorney. In 1894 Mr. Hicks resigned his office as district attorney and moved to San Antonio, where he was elected mayor, but he continued to practice law in various counties along the border until his death. Honorable Santos Benavides of Laredo was appointed district attorney to fill the unexpired term of Mr. Hicks and served until his resignation. He was followed by Honorable Sam Woods of Alice, Texas, who served as district attorney until 1897, when Honorable Arthur Claude Hamilton of Laredo was elected to that office. In 1902 Honorable John A. Valls of Laredo was elected district attorney. . . .
>
> Judge A. L. McLane served as district judge from the time of his appointment in 1891 until the early part of 1905, when he resigned. Governor Lanham appointed Honorable J. F. Mullally of Laredo as district judge, which office he held continuously until December 1938. It is of interest to note that Judge Mullally, as district judge, and Mr. Valls, as district attorney, worked together for more than thirty years, something we doubt is paralleled in any district of the state, if in the United States.

(167–168)

Fresh from their resounding election victory, Mullally and Valls set out the following day, Wednesday, November 6, 1912, to carry out the duties of their offices. The first order of business was empaneling the grand jury for the fall term of the court. Two days later, on November 8, the grand jury handed down the two indictments for murder against Alonzo W. Allee, and the following week, on November 12, the criminal docket of the Forty-ninth District Court for the fall term of 1912 was set for trial. According to the *Laredo Daily Times* of November 12, the less important cases, such as theft and burglary, were set for November 19 through November 21. The paper then added:

> There are two murder cases to be tried at this term of court, the Allee case and the San Miguel case, the latter being from Duval County. The setting of these cases will probably be made in the next day or so as soon as satisfactory agreements can be made between the prosecuting attorney and the counsel for the defense.

Three days later, on November 15, the newspaper reported that the two cases against Alonzo Allee had been set for December 10 and repeated that the defendant would be represented at trial by Hicks and Teargarden, while "District Attorney Valls will conduct the prosecution." Concurrently with setting the Allee cases for trial, Judge Mullally entered an order summoning two venires, or groups of prospective jurors, each composed of one hundred men. The newspaper added that each case (the murder of Francisco and the murder of Manuel) would be tried separately.

As for the district attorney, we can assume, from what is known about him, that John Valls was gearing up for battle in the upcoming trials. By all accounts he was an aggressive prosecutor, as well as a consummate politician and a colorful personage. A physical description of him gives an indication of the latter. Alicia Consuelo Worley, who in 1954 wrote her master's thesis on Valls, provides us the physical description of her subject from interviews with persons who knew him. According to Seb Wilcox, the court-reporter, Valls was "short and portly, with [a] ruddy complexion. His head [was] rather large for his body, and was slightly bald. In early days he wore a mustache to hide what he [Valls] called 'his bull dog mouth'—later he shaved it off" (Worley 93–94).

Worley also gives us his height as being five feet six inches and comments that Valls was somewhat of a dandy, devoting considerable care—and money—to his clothes: "It is said that he was so clothes conscious that he would change his suit twice a day. To top off his immaculate appearance he wore a carnation on his lapel daily" (95).

For being one of the Republican Party's standard bearers in Webb County, John Anthony Valls certainly had an unusual background. His father was a Spaniard from the island of Minorca who had emigrated as a young man and settled in New Orleans. In the United States the elder Valls anglicized his name to William, and in New Orleans he married a compatriot from Minorca, Evelina Valls, who, although she had the same surname, was no relation. When the Civil War came, William Valls served the Confederacy under General Pierre Beauregard. After the defeat of the South, William and Evelina Valls, like various other Southerners, moved to Mexico rather than live under the rule of Reconstruction. They settled in Bagdad, a small town at the mouth of the Rio Grande. There, on October 29, 1867, their son, John Anthony, was born.

A hurricane destroyed Bagdad in 1874, and the family then moved to Brownsville, Texas, just across the border. Valls was educated at Saint Joseph's School in Brownsville until he was fourteen, when he was sent to the Jesuit College at Spring Hill, near Mobile, Alabama. After graduating from Spring Hill, Valls began to study law at the University of Virginia at Charlottesville. By the age of twenty-one he had earned a law degree, and he returned to Brownsville to practice law for a short time. However, his family was undergoing financial difficulties at the time, and Valls looked outside Brownsville to improve the situation. Help came from a very powerful source. Mexico's president, General Porfirio Díaz, who occupied the presidency for thirty years, was godfather to John Anthony Valls, and he knew that a godfather had a responsibility to look after his godchild. (The Valls family had met General Díaz before he ascended the presidency, when the general was in Matamoros, across the river from Brownsville.) Through President Díaz the young Valls obtained the post of chief clerk in the central division of the Mexican National Railways in San Luis Potosí. Valls used his time in central Mexico to study Mexican law, and after some five years there he moved to Laredo, where he joined the law firm of C. C. Pierce.

In Laredo Valls worked hard practicing law, teaching English and

Latin in the public schools to augment his income, and making friends among the rich and powerful. His hard work paid off. In 1897 Valls was elected city attorney, in 1899 justice of the peace, and in 1902 he reached the office of district attorney, after defeating A. C. Hamilton with 2,022 votes to Hamilton's 1,146. The following election year, 1904, Valls defeated S. T. Phelps with 672 votes to Phelps's 77. In 1908 Valls had no opposition, but in 1912 Phelps again entered the fray, only to be trounced again (Worley 53–54).

Like his godfather, President Díaz, Valls remained in office through successive reelections that spanned several decades, and like Don Porfirio (as he was generally known), Valls did so through a profound knowledge of the uses and abuses of power. Valls knew when to attack and when to retreat, when to bend and when to stand firm. As the child of unreconstructed Southerners who became a successful politician in the Republican Party, John Valls was able to hold and reconcile opposing views and beliefs, which no doubt helped him to surmount the political crisis that he faced in the fall of 1912.

On Tuesday, November 19, 1912, the *Laredo Daily Times* reported the outcome of three cases tried before the empaneled petit jury in the district court. They were cases dealing with disturbing the peace, burglary, and assault with intent to murder; and in every case the result was a verdict of "not guilty." We do not know if the Webb County juries were remarkably disinclined to convict at this time or if the district attorney was not in good form in presenting these cases. The newspaper did not comment on the verdicts, so it is left to us to speculate about what was going on.

The next notice we have about the doings of the district court is the news story about the long-awaited Allee trials set for December 10. Since the *Laredo Daily Times* was an afternoon paper, it could carry the events of the morning on the same day. This was, in fact, one of the selling points used by the Penn Publishing Company in its own advertising: "Everything favors the afternoon newspaper for many reasons. After supper leisure is the logical time for the family circle to read the happenings of the day given in brief form."

After supper on Tuesday, December 10, the family circles in Laredo read that a delay had halted the proceedings in the Allee case that morning, but they were kept in suspense as to whether those proceedings had resumed in the afternoon, since the paper was probably put to bed shortly after twelve noon. The headline and the story that followed it read thus:

MATERIAL WITNESS ABSENT
Murder Case Called in District Court,
But Absence of Witness Caused a Slight Delay

This morning in the district court the two cases against Allee, charged with the killing of Francisco and Manuel Gutierrez on a ranch in this county several months ago, was called for trial before Judge Mullally, but owing to the absence of a material witness for the state a delay in the proceedings resulted.

The 200 special veniremen who had been summoned to appear this morning were present . . . the list of witnesses were called and it was then found that the state's most important witness had failed to arrive, but would reach here on this afternoon's Texas-Mexican train. A brief conference was held by the counsel for both sides and an agreement was reached whereby the procedure in the trial would be delayed a few hours. Judge Mullally announced that as a result of the agreement reached between counsel he would recess court until 4 o'clock this afternoon in order to allow the delinquent witness to put in his appearance.

Not only were the *Daily Times* readers left in suspense as to whether the "delinquent witness" had, indeed, put in an appearance that afternoon; they were also left wondering about the identity of the mysterious individual. The following day, December 11, the newspaper brought the answer to those questions but also raised new ones. The headline read: ONE OF MATERIAL WITNESSES FAILS TO APPEAR AND CASES SET FOR JANUARY 13. The story that followed gave the details:

The preliminary work of calling the list of 200 veniremen and the witnesses had been taken up when it was discovered that Ramon Medrano, alleged to be a material witness for the state, had failed to appear. . . .

Pursuant to adjournment court reconvened at 4 o'clock when all the veniremen and other witnesses appeared again, but the delinquent witness had failed to arrive on the train. Finally after some discussion as to a date that would be convenient to both sides for the trial of the case it was decided to set the cases for trial for January 13. The defendant is represented by Hicks and Hicks and Teargarden of San Antonio, while the prosecution is in charge of District Attorney Valls and the firm of Hamilton and Mann. . . .

Hon. Marshall Hicks, counsel for the defense, this morning stated that the first case which would be tried on January 13 would be that for the killing of Manuel Gutierrez, the younger man.

Unfortunately, the case record does not contain the list of witnesses subpoenaed by the state in the Allee cases in December 1912. However, the defendant's list of witnesses submitted by Marshall Hicks at that time still survives. Hicks subpoenaed some thirty-five men. About half of these were from outside Webb County, and we can only guess that the purpose of their testimony must have been to serve as character witnesses for the defendant, since they would have had no knowledge of the facts. Among the witnesses from Webb County, Hicks lists a Pedro Medrano. Pedro and Ramón Medrano may have been one and the same person, and the discrepancy in the names may have been an error of the newspaper. Or it may have been one person named Pedro Ramón Medrano (or vice versa), or they may have been two brothers—there are various possibilities. The most pressing questions, though, are: Who was Ramón/Pedro Medrano? Why was he referred to as "the state's most important witness," and why did both sides want his testimony? Only one person had witnessed the killing of Manuel Gutiérrez (that we know of), and that was Laureano Gutiérrez. Surely he was the state's most important witness.

Ramón Medrano was supposed to travel on the Texas-Mexican train that arrived in Laredo from Corpus Christi—after stops at points in between such as Aguilares—at 3:45 in the afternoon. Court recessed in the morning of December 10 until four o'clock that afternoon. The judge and both counselors clearly had a strong faith in the punctuality of the train schedules if they believed that Medrano would be at the Tex-Mex station at a quarter to four, in time to be quickly whisked away to the courthouse and into the courtroom by four. At any rate, the mystery witness did not arrive, and the result of his absence, according to the newspaper, was that the trial was postponed until the following year, set for January 13 of 1913.

Two other significant items are revealed in the same story, although no attention is called to them. The first is the reiteration of the names of counsel for each side, but now with an addition. The story now reads that the prosecution is in the charge of District Attorney Valls *and the firm of Hamilton and Mann.* The district attorney had seen fit or found it necessary to call in cocounsel for the Allee case.

The second significant item appears in the last paragraph, where the writer reported that Hon. Marshall Hicks, counsel for the defense, had announced that the first case to be tried on January 13 would be that of the killing of Manuel Gutiérrez. Scheduling decisions that may have repercussions on the conduct or the strategy of a trial are usually within the purview of the prosecution, unless the judge has ruled otherwise. Now Marshall Hicks appeared to be calling the shots in the case. Had something happened to cause the normally assertive district attorney to relinquish the central role that he clearly enjoyed playing in the judicial process?

A perusal of the *Laredo Daily Times* of some twelve days before— the issue of Friday, November 29, 1912—discloses, in a story tucked away on page 3, a possible and even probable reason for the district attorney's sudden reticence in the Allee case. The headline carried a humorous undertone and was cryptic in the extreme: REVOKES HIS DECISION: ASSISTANT ATTORNEY GENERAL FINALLY DISCOVERS THAT MR. VALLS IS DISTRICT ATTORNEY OF THIS DISTRICT. The story consisted almost entirely of the text of a letter, dated November 27, 1912, from O. C. Funderburk, assistant to the [Texas] attorney general, to Hon. Juan V. Benavides, county attorney of Webb County, and was in response to a question that Benavides had ostensibly asked the attorney general of the state. The question was: Did the Forty-ninth Judicial District of Texas have a district attorney?

The question must have exploded like a bomb at the feet of District Attorney Valls. Had he just been reelected by an overwhelming majority to an office that did not exist? Because the first answer that Assistant Attorney General Funderburk had given to Webb County Attorney Benavides was that such office did not exist. Then, in a second letter, he reversed his opinion. The rationale for Funderburk's first opinion, and for his subsequent reversal as well, describes such a labyrinthine legislative path that it defies paraphrasing. Only the full text of the letter can make it comprehensible—and only barely so:

Hon. Juan V. Benavides
County Attorney
Laredo, Texas

Dear Sir:
On the 23rd instant I wrote you in reply to an inquiry as to whether or not the office of District Attorney was lawfully in existence in the Forty-ninth Judicial District that in my opinion it was not.

Upon receipt of a letter today from Hon. John A. Valls, citing certain statutes, I am induced to re-consider the advice given you and to acknowledge that it was erroneous. In view of the fact that our highest courts after deciding a case ably presented by learned counsel on both sides by brief and argument, often find it necessary to recall and reverse its [sic] opinion, I need hardly apologize to you, a lawyer, for an error made in the rush of departmental business, where there has been no citation of authorities or argument made and nothing called to our attention emphasizing the importance of the question considered.

Section 5, Chapter 39, page 42, Acts 1891, organizing the 49th judicial district provides for the election of a district attorney in said district at subsequent elections. In the 1895 revision said Section 5, Acts 1891, was not brought forward but the same was saved from repeal by provision of Section 11 of the final title which reads as follows:

"That the laws now in force organizing the several judicial districts and prescribing the times of holding the district courts therein, are continued in force."

Chapter 58, page 80, Acts 1905 provides a reorganization of the 49th district, among others, and repeals all acts in conflict, but while providing that the then district attorney and district judges of the district reorganized shall serve "until the term of office for which each was elected may expire or until their successors have duly qualified," yet I am of opinion this provision was not in conflict with the said Section 5 of the Acts 1891 before referred to.

In the 1911 revision said section 11 of final title R.S. 1895 is brought forward, the effect of which being in my opinion, to keep in full force and effect the said provision in the Act of 1891 authorizing the election of district attorney in the 49th judicial district.

Yours very truly,
O. C. Funderburk, Assistant to Attorney General

A separate letter, also dated November 27, 1912, was addressed to District Attorney Valls and was, likewise, printed in the November 29 issue of the *Laredo Daily Times.*

Dear Sir:
Your letter of November 25, referring to our letter to the County Attorney of Webb County and citing certain statutes for our consideration is just received. We were in error in our opinion to the county attorney and are this day writing him to that effect, a copy of which we herewith enclose. I trust that the letter referred to has caused you no serious inconvenience.

Yours very truly,
O. C. Funderburk

The last sentence of the letter to the district attorney was surely ironic. We can be certain that after the first stunned moment of disbelief John Valls had immediately repaired to the law library to spend all his waking hours there, poring over the various tomes of session laws and statute books, looking for ammunition with which to refute the frightening possibility that loomed before him. It is not surprising, then, that the prosecution of burglary and assault cases at that time did not have the district attorney's full attention. What we must wonder, too, is whether the distraction of having to justify the existence of his office did not also cut into the time and effort that Valls would have allocated to preparing the prosecution of Alonzo Allee. Did the lack of preparation for the case lead Valls to posit the absence—or even the existence—of Ramón Medrano, the elusive witness, as a reason for obtaining a delay? Was the missing witness merely a way for Valls to save face for his lack of preparation and inability to go to trial? Or was there more to this imbroglio than meets the proverbial eye?

Some ten days before Funderburk's letter to Webb County Attorney Benavides, it was Webb County Sheriff Amador Sánchez who had been fighting to keep the office to which he had been so handily reelected on November 5. Only days after his overwhelming reelection, Amador Sánchez had found himself prevented from taking office by a temporary injunction granted by a district judge in San Antonio. The petitioner in this action was identified only as "the opponent of Sanchez" in the *Laredo Daily Times* issue of November 18, 1912. Since Sánchez had had five opponents in the election, the closest one receiving only fifty-three votes (and A. J. Barthelow, the former city marshal who had killed Alfred Allee, coming in last with one vote), the maneuver had all the earmarks of political partisan warfare. The reason given for enjoining Sánchez from qualifying for the office of sheriff was that "he had lost his citizenship when he pleaded guilty to a charge of violating the neutrality laws of the United States," according to the same issue of the *Daily Times.*

Of Amador Sánchez it can be said with justice that he had an "eventful career" (as opposed to a merely murderous one, like Alfred Allee). His biography appeared in *A Twentieth Century History of Southwest Texas,* and at the time of the book's publication, 1907, Amador Sánchez was mayor of Laredo and had been in that office since 1900 (78–79). He had begun his career in elective office in 1890 as district clerk of Webb County and remained in that position for three terms. After that he was elected sheriff and served as such until 1900, when he became mayor of Laredo. In 1910 he resigned from the mayor's office to return to being Webb County sheriff (Thompson 123).

This long, unbroken tenure in public office appeared no more unusual to Laredo voters than to the officeholder himself. Amador Sánchez descended from Captain Tomás Sánchez who, under the auspices of Don José de Escandón, founded Laredo in 1755. Captain Tomás Sánchez was also the son-in-law of Don José Vásquez Borrego, the largest landowner in the area that later became Webb and Zapata Counties. Thus, the Sánchez descendants, having both the pedigree and the wealth, were the natural leaders of Laredo, even in the face of the growing Anglo influence.

But Amador Sánchez did not merely rest on the laurels of his background. He was also a well-educated man and an enterprising one. He had graduated from Saint Mary's University in Galveston, Texas, where he received "a most liberal education" and was by profession a civil engineer, according to his biography (79). At that time most wealth in South Texas and the border area was based on land, and here again the sheriff's accomplishments were impressive. According to *A Twentieth Century History of Southwest Texas,* "he [Sánchez] and his associates now [1907] have in the state of Tamaulipas, a stock ranch of 100,000 acres. Mr. Sanchez has also for many years been extensively interested in various mining enterprises in the Republic of Mexico." Regarding the sheriff's political achievements, the biographer added: "He has for many years been a prominent figure in the Democratic party in the state of Texas. He was chairman of the Democratic executive committee of Webb County for four years, and a member of the Democratic state executive committee for a similar period" (79).

Although Sheriff Amador Sánchez and District Attorney John A. Valls belonged to rival political parties, they shared remarkable similarities: they were both not only prominent in the affairs of their own parties, but each could be described as the standard bearer for his party in Webb County. In addition, both men were highly educated professionals with business and personal connections in two countries. Finally, they were both staunch *porfiristas* (supporters of Mexican president Porfirio Díaz), or at least ardent anti-*maderistas* (as in Francisco Madero, who overthrew Díaz), during the Mexican Revolution of 1910.

The Rio Grande might have become the dividing line between the United States and Mexico in 1848, but the lands bordering the river had all been one country for some three hundred years before that. The same families had settled both sides of the river for about one hundred years before the Treaty of Guadalupe Hidalgo. Laredo and, to a lesser extent, the rest of Webb County continued to look toward Mexico as much, if not more, as toward the United States in political and economic matters. District Attorney Valls himself had been born in Mexico and probably retained dual citizenship. Valls's biographer, Worley, recounts that President Porfirio Díaz had offered the young lawyer the post of Mexican consul in Brownsville, Texas, but Valls had declined to take it, since he would have had to renounce his United States citizenship (22). Accepting an official post with the Mexican government would have certainly resulted in Valls forfeiting his United States citizenship, but this does not imply that Valls would have needed to become a Mexican citizen in order to be a Mexican consul. Valls was already a Mexican citizen by birth.

In November 1912 it was Sheriff Sánchez's citizenship that was in question, according to the *Laredo Daily Times.* This was not exactly accurate. It was not his citizenship that was at issue; it was his right to vote and hold office. These are lost after a criminal conviction. Earlier in the same year, on January 8, Amador Sánchez had been indicted in the federal district court for the Southern District of Texas for violation of the Neutrality Laws, had pleaded guilty, and had been sentenced to pay a fine of twelve hundred dollars (Thompson 123).

The Neutrality Laws, which had been on the books since the end of the eighteenth century, were being invoked rather frequently in the early part of the twentieth in response to activities carried out in the United States but aimed at Mexico. By 1910 the presidency of General Porfirio Díaz, which had spanned over thirty years, was tottering on its foundations. For a long time the general, now in his eighties, had successfully fought off rivals and foes while opening Mexico to foreign investment and spurring economic development. Prosperity at the top, though, had not trickled down to the native masses, and by 1910 the grievances arising from years of political and physical oppression had coalesced around an opposition movement. This opposition was led— reluctantly at first—by Francisco I. Madero, the scion of one of the wealthiest and most prominent families in the northern Mexican state of Coahuila.

Madero, under threat of arrest in Mexico for his political activities, had fled to the United States and established himself in San Antonio, from which he communicated with a variety of sympathizers while they plotted to overthrow the Díaz regime. Madero's activities in the United States displeased not only the Mexican government but also many public and private individuals in the States, and finally, in February 1911, Madero returned to Mexico, crossing the border at El Paso just in time to escape a federal arrest warrant for violation of the Neutrality Laws (Cumberland 128–129). The first shot of the Mexican Revolution was fired on November 20, 1910, but it was not until the end of May 1911 that it became clear that the people of Mexico were tired of Don Porfirio and his government, and the old general, facing countrywide rebellion, tendered his resignation and left for the port of Veracruz to board a ship bound for France. An interim government followed that called for a presidential election, and on November 6, 1911, Francisco I. Madero was elected president of Mexico and José María Pino Suárez vice-president (Cumberland 170).

It was soon clear that the only thing that had held together many of the revolutionaries had been an anti-Díaz sentiment. With Díaz gone, factions developed that flared up into rebellion. A year later, in the fall of 1912, Madero became an embattled president, trying to suppress insurrections led by both former supporters and by counterrevolutionaries who were trying to resurrect the *porfiriato* (as the Díaz regime and era were known). The Díaz regime may have been oppressive to its own people, but it had also been brutally efficient in maintaining law and order; and foreign investors, particularly those from the United States, bitterly resented Madero for the chaos that he and his movement unleashed. Newspapers in the United States, including the *Laredo Daily Times*, constantly castigated Madero, reporting on frequent depredations by Mexican rebels or bandits—the two terms were often used interchangeably—and blaming the new government for the instability.

The *Laredo Weekly Times* of September 29, 1912, for example, reported on the difficulties that the Blocker brothers, John and Walter, were having with their operations in Mexico: "One thousand rebels, claiming to be under Orozco's command [General Pascual Orozco, a former ally of Madero who had rebelled against him], are encamped opposite here [Langtry, Texas] in Mexico. J. R. and Walter Blocker, American cattlemen, coming here today from importing cattle, claimed that these rebels charged them export duty in the name of the Orozco government."

It was for one of these rebellions against President Madero that Sheriff Amador Sánchez was indicted. This particular rebellion was led by General Bernardo Reyes, a former governor of the state of Nuevo León who had hoped to succeed Porfirio Díaz as president and who was now allied with Díaz's nephew against Madero. General Reyes, like Madero and others before him, also tried to lay the groundwork for his rebellion from inside United States territory. This was not so strange, since there was no better place to acquire arms and war materiel than across the northern border, particularly in Texas.

> As early as August, 1911, before the Mexican election, Major Hagadorn, commanding Fort McIntosh, reported the presence of Reyista arms in Laredo. By November, Hagadorn and Mr. Stover, head of the U.S. Immigration Service in Laredo, had developed that the arms were stored in the Webb County jail and in a number of houses. . . . Horses and saddles also were concentrated

near Laredo for the use of Reyista soldiers and filibusters. Hagadorn seized a house in which he found the captain and 15 men of a company raised for duty in Reyes' revolution, 40 rifles, 20,000 rounds of ammunition, and 50 bombs presumably made of dynamite stolen from the coal mines at Minera. Three days later Reyes' horses were confiscated. Reyes was in Laredo, and both he and the Webb County sheriff were indicted for violation of the Neutrality Act and released on bond.   (WILKINSON 383)

Sheriff Sánchez had pleaded guilty, paid his fine, and probably considered that he had discharged his debt to society until the matter was resurrected in the aftermath of his resounding victory. When the issue did surface in such dramatic form, Amador Sánchez turned to fellow Democrat Marshall Hicks, or at least to his firm, to represent him. After responding to the action for an injunction, which was heard in San Antonio, Sheriff Sánchez and B. W. Teargarden, his attorney (of Hicks and Hicks and Teargarden), proceeded to Austin to meet with Governor Oscar B. Colquitt, another Democrat, who apparently reassured them that the matter was not fatal, particularly in light of the statewide Democratic sweep of the recent elections. The *Laredo Daily Times* of November 18, 1912, reported:

> Sheriff Amador Sanchez, who left here [Laredo] several days ago for Austin to meet and confer with Governor Colquitt to avert the injunction enjoining him from qualifying as sheriff, returned to Laredo this morning. Regarding his visit to the state capital, an Austin dispatch published in yesterday's papers contains the following:
>
> Amador Sanchez, who was reelected Sheriff of Webb County at the recent election, but who was enjoined from qualifying on the grounds that he lost his citizenship when he pleaded guilty to a charge of violating the neutrality laws of the United States, arrived here today from Laredo, accompanied by his attorney, B. W. Teargarden of San Antonio.
>
> The two conferred with Governor Colquitt. Contention is made by Sanchez that the action brought against him at San Antonio is irregular for the reason that no authority has been

given for bringing the application in the name of the State of
Texas; that the application was filed by the opponent of Sanchez.

The result of the conference was not made public, Sanchez and his lawyer leaving this afternoon for San Antonio.
Both expressed themselves confident that Sanchez will be duly
installed in office.

Just because two events happen contemporaneously, or even in se-
quence, does not mean that they are related, much less that it is a question of cause and effect. However, in the suffocatingly close political en-
vironment of South Texas in 1912, particularly in Webb County, the fact
that the two most prominent officeholders—the sheriff and the district
attorney—who were members of rival political parties, were embroiled
in challenges to their reelection, one because he allegedly was ineligible
to hold office and the other because there was no office to hold, does
give rise to a whiff of causality, or, more precisely, of tit for tat. The scenario that emerges is one in which the Republicans try to make hay out
of the sheriff's troubles with the federal government by attempting to
enjoin him from serving another term, and the Democrats retaliate by
attacking the Republican district attorney, not personally but as an
officeholder without an office.

When Sheriff Amador Sánchez found himself in trouble, he ap-
plied to a fellow Democrat, Marshall Hicks, for legal assistance, and
Hicks was able and, no doubt, glad to oblige. Hicks's political creden-
tials were even more impressive than his legal ones, and the latter were
not negligible. He had served on the Democratic State Executive Committee, just like Amador Sánchez, but he had also been "chairman of
the State Democratic Convention at Waco in 1900. In 1912 . . . he was
delegate at large to the Democratic National Convention at Baltimore"
(Wharton 17). Hicks had also represented the Twenty-fourth Senatorial
District of Texas from 1903 to 1907, which meant that in 1912 he would
still have had friends in Austin, especially in those days of lower turn-
over in state offices. But, even more compellingly, Marshall Hicks had
been the first district attorney of the Forth-ninth Judicial District, appointed to the post by his patron, Governor Jim Hogg, and was therefore
thoroughly cognizant of the terms of the legislation creating the district. Furthermore, Hicks had been in the Texas Senate when the Texas
Legislature crafted legislation for the reorganization of the Forty-ninth
District. Who better than Hicks, then, to raise skillful doubts as to the

status of the district attorney's office, especially after the legislative mill was through grinding? Hicks himself did not question the status of the office, of course. It would have been unseemly. The proper conduit for the challenge was the Webb County attorney, Juan V. Benavides, another Democrat.

A historian would undoubtedly have given much to be the proverbial fly on the wall in Governor Colquitt's office when Sheriff Sánchez and his lawyer, B. W. Teargarden, visited with him. The same fly might have then followed the two visitors to the attorney general's office, where they would have discussed the disposition of the Webb County attorney's question regarding the district attorney's office. A brilliant strategy would have been sketched out at that time: first a resounding "No" as to whether John Valls had an office to fill; then, when they had his attention and Valls was thoroughly rattled, a retraction in exchange for—what? Dropping the Sánchez persecution and a more accommodating prosecution of the Allee case which occupied Hicks at the time? If, in addition to checkmating the Republicans in the matter of the sheriff's reelection, Marshall Hicks also gained an advantage in the Allee trial, so much the better. It was a win-win situation—for Marshall Hicks.

Alonzo Allee's trial had been continued until January 13, 1913, and the court convened on that day, as planned. We can assume that the same two hundred (more or less) prospective jurors of the previous December also put in an appearance. Marshall Hicks had already subpoenaed several witnesses in addition to the thirty-seven that he had called for December 10. Among those witnesses was Lee Henrichson of La-Salle County, probably the same person as R. L. Henrichsen, who had been one of the sureties on Allee's bond. Other witnesses were "Capt. T. M. Ross" and "Wm. Ross, Jr.," identified as stockmen of Atascosa County; W. T. Brite, farmer, of Atascosa County; and Jessie Fleming of Bexar County, described as "Boarder—girl." The purpose of calling such persons must have been to secure testimony as to Allee's good character, but we never find out, because when Hicks appeared in court that morning it was to ask for a delay until two o'clock that afternoon. He claimed that he needed the additional time to produce an important witness for the defense. When two o'clock came, though, Hicks came to court, not with the missing witness, but with a motion for a change of venue. This maneuver is an example of what came to be known as trial by ambush.

On January 14 the *Laredo Daily Times* reported:

When district court reconvened yesterday afternoon following
the morning recess, during which time the defense were supposed to secure the attendance of absent witnesses, the counsel
for defense made an application for a change of venue, the
grounds for this action being the allegation that prejudice against
the defense existed in this community and that a fair and impartial jury could not be secured. This precipitated a new phase and
accordingly argument pro and con along those lines resulted.

The application for a change of venue contained in the case records
consisted of affidavits sworn to and signed by the defendant, Alonzo W.
Allee, and by R. W. Roberson and W. Y. Bunn. Allee's affidavit read:

Now comes Alonzo W. Allee, the defendant in the above
entitled cause, and states under oath that there exists in this,
Webb County, so great a prejudice against him that he can not
obtain a fair and impartial trial of this cause in said county.
　　　Wherefore, he asks the Court to change the venue of this
cause to some county that is free from this and other objections.

That this maneuver had been planned in advance by defense counsel Hicks and that it came as a surprise to the district attorney can be
deduced from the technology of the times. The defendant's affidavits for
a change of venue are completely typewritten, except for the names of
Roberson and Bunn, which are filled in by hand, indicating that the two
were probably chosen that same day from among the defendant's witnesses and other well-wishers in attendance at the courthouse. The district attorney's opposing affidavit, however, is handwritten, leading to
the conclusion that it was hastily drafted, since the district attorney's
office surely possessed at least one typewriter.
　　　Roberson and Bunn's joint affidavit recited that they were residents
of Webb County, that they were informed of the contents of the application for a change of venue filed by Alonzo Allee, and that "there does
exist in said Webb County, Texas, so great a prejudice against Alonzo W.
Allee, defendant, that he can not obtain a fair and impartial trial."
　　　In his opposing affidavit, District Attorney Valls refuted the defense contention that Alonzo Allee could not receive a fair trial in Webb

County and challenged Roberson and Bunn's factual basis for making that contention:

> Affiant [Valls] further states that the means of knowledge of defendant's compurgators [Roberson and Bunn] upon whose affidavit the change of venue is sought in this cause, are imperfect touching the prejudice alleged to exist in said county and their conclusion that the defendant Alonzo W. Allee cannot get a fair and impartial trial in Webb County, Texas, are not true in fact and their means of knowledge and information on the question of prejudice against Alonzo W. Allee in said county are not sufficient to authorize the making of said affidavit. [Signed] John A. Valls, District Attorney.

There followed, according to the January 14 issue of the *Laredo Daily Times*, testimony on both sides:

> The defense summoned a number of creditable witnesses by whom they sought to establish their contention and the examination of these witnesses consumed most of the afternoon [of January 13]. The prosecution likewise summoned a number of prominent citizens to prove their contention that a competent and impartial jury was obtainable here. The investigation continued until about 10 o'clock this morning [January 14], during which time quite a number expressed their views on the subject.

Marshall Hicks had clearly come to court prepared with his typewritten affidavits and his witnesses ready to testify about "so great a prejudice" against his client. Since the defense was the movant or petitioner for the change of venue, it had the burden of proving its case. Hicks called as witnesses to support Allee's claim of prejudice the following: the affiants, R. W. Roberson and W. Y. Bunn, Ed Cotulla, Ira T. Pence, D. N. Cobb, and A. J. Landrum. The last one, Landrum, was the original lessee of La Volanta, the person who had leased the ranch from Francisco Gutiérrez in May 1911 and who had presumably subleased it later to Allee, in contravention of state law.

The testimony of these witnesses was not recorded or, most likely, it was recorded by Seb Wilcox, the court reporter, but not transcribed and preserved. In those days court reporters took down testimony in shorthand, using any of the standard methods, but occasionally they developed their own particular eclectic system, which made it impossible for anyone else to transcribe their notes. In any case, this particular testimony was not preserved, and we are left to imagine what Allee's witnesses could have alleged in court to demonstrate that prejudice existed against him in Webb County.

Allee's arrest had not produced popular outrage against the accused, as had been present with the arrests of Lonnie Franks and James Barney Compton, the murderers of Levytansky, the jeweler. To the contrary, Allee had received the utmost consideration, being quietly transported to jail by Deputy Sheriff Hill, his old companion. Sureties had stood by ready to post his bond, so that he was promptly released. And he had first-class legal representation, not a court-appointed lawyer. It was not Alonzo Allee as an individual who feared not receiving a fair trial, therefore, but Allee as a member of the Anglo American minority of Webb County who claimed prejudice.

But upon what particular basis, apart from the generalized tension between Anglos and Mexicans throughout the state, could this contention be made in Webb County? E. A. Tarver had claimed in the previously cited article that the Laredo Mexicans were generously sharing political offices with the Anglo minority. What had the Mexicans done, then, to raise Anglo fears of prejudice, or what incident could be used as a pretext to make such a claim? One example that Allee's witnesses could have made reference to was a gathering held in Laredo from September 14 through September 22, 1911, which was known as El Primer Congreso Mexicanista (The First Mexicanist Congress) (Limón 86). The Congreso had been organized by Nicasio Idar, publisher of *La Crónica*, a Spanish-language newspaper in Laredo, as well as the justice of the peace who conducted the first investigation into the killing of the Gutiérrez men.

Nicasio Idar's influence in Laredo did not derive from membership in the leading families, as was the case with Sheriff Amador Sánchez and County Attorney Juan V. Benavides. Idar was an outsider, like District Attorney Valls, but unlike Valls, Idar did not become part of the political establishment of Webb County, although he served at different times as assistant city marshal and justice of the peace (Limón 87). Today Idar would be described as a community activist, one who used the power of the press to try to better the lot of his fellow Mexicans.

Nicasio Idar was born in 1853 in Point Isabel, Texas, near Brownsville and not too far, either, from old Bagdad, Tamaulipas, the birthplace of John A. Valls. He moved to Laredo in 1880, after living in Corpus Christi and attending school there (Limón 87). By occupation he was a commercial printer. His interest in political events and his concern for the welfare of the Mexican residents of Texas led him to crusading journalism and to publish various newspapers with the help of three of his eight children—Clemente, Eduardo, and Jovita. *La Crónica* is the best known of these publications.

On February 2, 1911, Idar had called, through *La Crónica,* for a general meeting of a fraternal order that he had been instrumental in organizing, La Orden Caballeros de Honor. This meeting led to the convocation of the Primer Congreso Mexicanista. The impetus for this convocation was manifold, as were the individuals who were to be invited to participate.

On the front page of *La Crónica* Idar began by inviting all Mexican journalists in Texas to attend, as well as "todos los mexicanos más ilustrados en las letras, residentes en Texas" ("all the prominent Mexican men and women of letters residing in Texas"), the Mexican consuls, and all those persons interested in the general welfare "de nuestra raza en este país" ("of our people in this country").

Among the topics to be broached during the Congreso were the following: (1) the exclusion of Mexican children from public schools in some parts of Texas; (2) the need to teach the Spanish language and the establishment of schools staffed by degreed teachers brought from Mexico to do so; (3) discussion of means to assure improved protection of the lives and interests of Mexicans; (4) the forming of women's auxiliary organizations affiliated with the Order of Caballeros; and (5) the need for Mexicans to acquire more property and to retain the property they already had in Texas.

The last provision must have sent shivers down the spines of the ranchers, farmers, and real estate developers in South Texas who in the early part of the twentieth century were busily acquiring more land from Mexicans who did not exploit or realize its full potential. For example, on February 11, 1915, the *Brownsville Daily Herald* carried the following story, headed: MANY CAPITALISTS ARE BUYING LANDS IN THE LOWER VALLEY. The story continued:

Floyd Shock, president and general manager of the Missouri-Texas Land & Irrigation Company, with headquarters in St. Louis

Missouri, is in San Antonio, returning from Hidalgo County, where the company controls 60,000 acres of land in the Rio Grande Valley.

Mr. Shock says much St. Louis capital is being invested in that section of Texas and instances the purchase of thousands of acres by millionaires of the Missouri metropolis. . . . It is interesting to note this land not so many years ago was sold for 50 cents an acre. Now none of it is selling for less than $50 an acre.

The reference to assuring the protection of the lives of Mexicans was undoubtedly understood by the readers of *La Crónica* as relating to a gruesome event that had taken place in Rocksprings, Texas, on November 2, 1910. On that day, reported *La Crónica* in the issue of November 12, a twenty-year-old Mexican man named Antonio Rodríguez had been accused of the murder of an Anglo woman, Mrs. Lem Henderson, at a ranch near "Rock Springs," in Edwards County, northwest of San Antonio. The residents of Rocksprings had not waited for the niceties of the legal process to establish Rodríguez's guilt. He had been taken from the jail by a mob who tied him to a tree and burned him to death.

The incident, when reported by the press in Mexico, provoked anti-American demonstrations in Mexico City, which, in turn, provoked anti-Mexican denunciations in the United States newspapers. Idar had reported reluctantly on these events on November 12, 1910, explaining that *La Crónica* carried the story because the public was anxious to learn the details, although the philosophy of the newspaper led it to eschew stories relating to crime ("Muy triste es para nosotros consignar estos hechos que horrorizan, máxime cuando nos hemos propuesto no publicar noticias de crímenes en nuestro periódico; pero el público está ansioso por conocer los detalles").

In any case, the Primer Congreso Mexicanista had not left any dire consequences in its wake for the Anglo residents of South Texas; and, despite its name, which indicated the expectation of at least a second Congreso, the event had not been repeated as of January 1913.

Alonzo Allee had not been in fear of being lynched by a mob of outraged Laredoans. He had been out on bail since August 1912, a few days after he killed Francisco and Manuel Gutiérrez. However, Allee, or, more precisely, his defense counsel, Marshall Hicks, was certainly conscious of the fact that, with the majority of Laredoans being of Mexican origin in whole or in part, the victims in this case would certainly receive much more sympathy in Laredo than elsewhere in Texas.

Surely, though, the defense witnesses at the hearing on the application for a change of venue would not have made explicit the fear that the Mexicans (if any) on the Allee jury would retaliate against Allee for his and his fellow Anglos' crimes against Mexicans. Marshall Hicks undoubtedly coached them to be more subtle in their testimony, but the underlying message would have been there.

For his part, District Attorney Valls did not take lightly the defense's challenge to his prerogative to try the case. He brought out heavy ammunition to refute the application. Among the state's witnesses, Valls called the mayor of Laredo, Robert McComb; the superintendent of schools, L. J. Christen; and other leaders of the community, such as Quintín Villegas, an uncle of Leopoldo, the foreman of the grand jury that had indicted Allee; P. P. Leyendecker; A. M. Bruni, the county treasurer and a wealthy rancher with extensive land holdings around Aguilares, in the southeastern part of the county; H. Ligarde; Eugene Christen, and others. They all testified, according to the *Laredo Daily Times*, that Webb County could provide fair and impartial juries to hear the murder cases against Alonzo Allee.

District Judge John F. Mullally, who presided at the hearing, agreed with the state and denied the defendant's motion for a change of venue.

Still, Marshall Hicks secured the objective that, most likely, had been his goal all along: to have the trial postponed again—this time until the next term of the court, which began in May, four months later.

With the Allee case temporarily out of the way, the community leaders of Laredo could now turn their attention to planning the most important civic and social event of the city: the celebration of George Washington's birthday in February. How this event came to be the focal point of the Laredo social calendar has been described before, including by Falvella in his text to the *Official Souvenir Program*, written for the seventeenth George Washington's Birthday Celebration, in 1916. Falvella and others attribute the first celebration to members of a lodge, the Improved Order of Red Men. According to Falvella, one of the lodge members suggested that "inasmuch as the 'Red Men' were the real aborigines of the United States, that their ritual was strictly along the principles of American life of the long ago . . . that it was befitting the Red Men to celebrate the natal day anniversary of that stalwart Virginian" (15).

The "Red Men" were, of course, the leading businessmen and public officials that Falvella featured in his other 1916 publication, the *Souvenir Album of Laredo*. The Red Men began the George Washington's Birthday Celebration every year with a mock attack on the city hall, which was defended by police and public officials. The battle raged facetiously until those under siege capitulated and presented the keys to the city to the Princess Pocahontas. All were friends then and together proceeded to celebrate with a grand parade, carnivals, and street fairs. If we add that District Judge J. F. Mullally, as a young attorney, had been secretary of the Red Men chapter in Laredo when it initiated the Washington's Birthday celebrations, it may give an idea of the social and civic prominence of the event (Young, "Red Men" 57).

Why George Washington's birthday was celebrated in such elaborate fashion in a town founded by Spanish Creoles before the United States came into being is still open to interpretation, but we have some clues. As has been mentioned before, after the Treaty of Guadalupe Hidalgo Laredoans had petitioned the governments of both countries to be allowed to remain part of Mexico. The United States refused, and more Anglos began trickling down to settle on that part of the border. Whether the newcomers knew the story of the petition or not, the Anglos could not have failed to notice where the sympathies and affection of old Laredoans lay, and, undoubtedly taken aback by this lack of enthusiasm for being "American," they eventually devised a means to Americanize the old town. Americanizing Laredo was not a simple matter, according to Elliott Young, a historian, who explains that the process could not be accomplished "through a direct imposition of Anglo American culture, symbols and values. The historic, geographic, and demographic significance of Mexico and Mexicans on the border had to be incorporated into the very concept of America" (Young, "Red Men" 50).

But why was February 22, George Washington's birthday, picked as the date and event to celebrate, as opposed to, for example, the Fourth of July? Anyone who has spent a summer in South Texas will be quick to answer that the weather must have been the deciding factor. Late February in that area is generally cool and almost springlike, more conducive to enjoying parades and outdoor festivities than the sweltering temperatures of July. As a matter of fact, the *Laredo Daily Times* of February 19, 1913, touted the mildness of the weather as a reason for the success of the celebration, year after year:

For a number of years Laredo has celebrated the anniversary of the illustrious Washington in a manner which has been the envy of many a larger city throughout the country. The climate, of course, aided a great deal in the celebration. . . . And people from far and near—residents of Texas, residents of Monterrey and intermediary points, northern people who were spending a few winter months at San Antonio and other Texas winter resorts— all came, saw and were conquered. Nowhere else do they find such charming, all-embracing hospitality. Nowhere else can they dress as for summer at home and enjoy the mildness of the Laredo climate.

Late February often coincides, as well, with carnival festivities among Latin peoples, which would predispose the native Laredo population to celebrate. The whole point of the exercise was to prepare a receptive audience for the Americanization process. However, more than a hundred years of a common history and continued shared experiences cannot be erased, and so, along with tableaux depicting "Washington Crossing the Delaware" and decorated floats portraying "Life in Old Virginia," the Washington's Birthday celebrations came to include bullfights in Nuevo Laredo by 1913. The George Washington's Birthday Celebration, begun as an effort to incorporate Laredo into the American way of life, had by 1913 become a celebration of the continued interdependence of the two cities and the two countries, a celebration of the particular hybrid way of life on the border.

In 1913 George Washington's Birthday Celebration spanned the weekend of Friday, February 21; Saturday, February 22; and Sunday, February 23, with the grandest events concentrated on Saturday. The highlight of the festivities was the parade held on Saturday, February 22. The parade committee chairman that year was Eugene Christen, the fire marshal, who had been a member of the grand jury during the fall term of the district court. The *Laredo Daily Times* of February 10, 1913, reported that that year the parade would include "a greater number of decorated vehicles and automobiles . . . while the showing made by the decorated trade displays will be more elaborate than heretofore."

One constant—and surely unique—feature of the parade every year was the participation of Princess Pocahontas and her escort, Captain John Smith, a masterstroke in that milieu where people accepted the mixing of Europeans and Indians. Pocahontas was usually portrayed by a young lady of the best Laredo society—preferably one who could ride a horse. That year, the *Times* announced on February 10, the role of the Indian princess would be taken by Miss Lila Randolph, who would be "attired in a robe made of real buckskin and secured from a manufacturer of wearing apparel for Indians."

In 1913 word of the elaborate festivities in Laredo had spread to Hollywood, and Universal Film Company was expected to be present to record the colorful events, according to the *Daily Times* of February 7. To coincide with the 1913 celebration, the International & Great Northern Railway had inaugurated a new station in Laredo, the newspaper also reported. In order to house the influx of visitors, persons having "rooms, beds or cots" were asked to notify the lodging committee or City Marshal Brennan. Visitors were expected to arrive on trains that reached Laredo from three directions—north, south, and east. The *Laredo Daily Times* of Friday, February 21, reported that the International & Great Northern, which came from San Antonio, and the Texas-Mexican, which traveled from Corpus Christi, had brought "excursionists from their terminals and intermediate points, there being fully 1,000 people on both trains."

The only setback to the celebration was the disappointment that the expected excursionists from Monterrey did not arrive. By February 22 the Mexican National Railroad's train was not running to Laredo. Train service along that route and others in Mexico had been interrupted after lines had been blown up by various rebel forces. The Mexican Revolution had begun in earnest.

The *Laredo Daily Times* found itself in a quandary. The news of the uprising and coup d'état against President Madero in Mexico represented an embarrassment of riches for news copy, but it posed a grave threat to the success of the Washington's Birthday Celebration. The paper tried to juggle both stories, while at the same time editorializing against rumormongering and panic. On Wednesday, February 19, the *Daily Times* had admonished its readers:

> Such idle, senseless rumors as those which have been circulated through the mails, over the telephones and by telegraph messages are potential injuries to our city and its energetic organizations who have done so much to build up our annual fiesta. From assurances by the authorities on the other side of the river,

we feel certain in stating that there is not the slightest need for apprehension. Officials of Nuevo Laredo state that they will do all in their power to make the celebration a success as they have done in the past. With the peaceful surrender of the garrisons in New [sic] Laredo and Matamoros to the new regime and the statement that Mr. Madero has decided to accept his defeat without further bloodshed, there is no reason to fear any hostile action towards Americans who wish to cross over the great International bridge and explore the town.

It is difficult not to wonder if Justo S. Penn, the publisher of the *Times,* did not realize the incongruity of his assurances to his readers, in light of the telegram from Webb County Sheriff Amador Sánchez to Governor Colquitt, which the *Times* had published only four days before, on February 15. The telegram read:

Hon. O. B. Colquitt, Governor, Austin, Texas. A large number of rebels headed by Col. Andres Garza Galan, Nicanor Valdez and Pascual Orozco, Sr., took Nuevo Laredo, just across the river, this afternoon. The garrison, composed of about 250 volunteers and 150 federal soldiers, joined Garza Galan proclaiming General [Gerónimo] Treviño as president of Mexico. The customs house, municipal palace and all other public buildings are in hands of rebels. Order prevails at present. I communicated at once with leader of rebels, requesting them not to fire across the border, as this action may bring international complications. Col. Garza Galan promised me they would not fire across the line. People on this side quiet. Wire instructions. Amador Sanchez, Sheriff.

Two days later, on Monday, February 17, 1913, the *Laredo Daily Times* published a synopsis of the "Situation in Nuevo Laredo:"

While everything is quiet . . . the conditions are as follows: Rebel forces in charge of Garza Galan have received a number of recruits. Sunday afternoon, the rebel army, accompanied by the bugle corps and municipal band, paraded through the streets of Nuevo Laredo. Sunday evening hundreds of women and children abandoned their homes in Nuevo Laredo and came across to this city to make their temporary residence. Women and children and aged men were allowed to leave, but by order of the military commander, all men between 16 and 60 were ordered detained and not allowed to leave. The sheriff's office and the commander at Fort McIntosh have stationed guards on the U.S. side of the international bridge while on the Mexican side of the bridge a large force of soldiers is constantly on guard. Business generally has resumed normal conditions [but] conductors, engineers, and firemen on the National lines and who were in Nuevo Laredo or Laredo this morning quit work in a body and refused to operate the trains. . . . [T]he National Railways of Mexico have abandoned all train service southward out of Laredo [and employees] deserted their positions this morning and according to what the *Times* reporter has learned, most of them have come to this city to remain pending an improvement of the situation. The Western Union operators in Nuevo Laredo abandoned their jobs, and the men are now [in Laredo, Texas].

Surely this sudden influx of refugees from Nuevo Laredo strained the availability of lodging in Laredo, taking up the rooms, beds and cots needed to house the excursionists arriving later that week to celebrate. If so, the *Daily Times* forbore to say it, partially out of neighborliness, but also to avoid discouraging the arrival of the expected merrymakers. In a last desperate effort to reassure prospective visitors to the Washington's Birthday celebration, the newspaper announced peace on Thursday, February 20, under the headline CONDITIONS PEACEABLE IN NUEVO LAREDO.

Send the good news that all is now serene on the Rio Grande, that the incipient revolution . . . has vanished like the mythical thing it was and tranquility . . . prevails. This morning a large force of men put to work repairing damage to the railway and in a day or two through trains from Mexico City to Laredo and viceversa will be in operation, mail service will be re-established and the transportation facilities thus afforded will mean a resumption of the wheels of commerce that have been idle in the past week.

That Friday, February 21, news of the revolution in Mexico was banished from the front page of the *Laredo Daily Times*. The inside pages contained only short reports on the Mexican situation from the Associated Press under the headline NEW REVOLUTIONS CROPPING UP: MADERO'S FATE TAKES SECOND PLACE IN INTEREST AS HIS DEATH IS NOT LIKELY EVENT. The story reported that United States Ambassador Henry Lane Wilson, who had taken an active hand in bringing about President Madero's downfall, had sent a cable to Washington in which he assured the State Department that Madero would "neither be thrown into a madhouse [as proposed earlier] nor summarily executed, but [would] be given a fair trial, and . . . his worst possible fate [would] be exile."

The stories of revolution in Mexico were not allowed to compete with happy descriptions of the Washington's Birthday celebrations carried that weekend by the *Laredo Daily Times,* but by Monday, February 24, the bad news could not be concealed any longer. The headline on the front page proclaimed, MURDERED MADERO AND PINO SUAREZ, and on the following day, February 25, Justo S. Penn felt compelled to publish in the *Daily Times* an editorial that read like a fiery sermon, under the headline A WILFUL MURDER.

> There is no other characterization for the slayings of Francisco Madero and Jose Pino Suarez. . . . Whatever the outcome of the present movement, there can be no doubt in the minds of any that the assassinations of Madero and Suarez has indelibly stained the present government [headed by General Victoriano Huerta, Madero's chief of staff, who betrayed him]. A government founded upon assassination cannot long exist. It bears within itself the seeds of approaching dissolution. It is already foul with the corruption of the grave. . . . Madero living was not formidable to even his foes. But Madero dead . . . and dead through treachery, is a ghost which, like that of Banquo, will rise up at times unsuspected and thwart the plans of those who sent him to cross the dark river. Even his enemies could wish a kinder fate for the late president of Mexico. And his friends will not only mourn, but avenge his untimely death.

Not even Justo S. Penn himself could have imagined how prophetic his words would turn out to be. It would be at least five years before some kind of tranquility could be restored to Mexico, and Laredo would share in the turmoil of those times.

With revolutions and carnivals in the early months of 1913, did anyone in Laredo, besides the families of the victims, remember that justice was still to be done in the killings of Francisco and Manuel Gutiérrez? Sheriff Amador Sánchez, for one, had turned his mind to happier things. On February 21, 1913, coinciding with the Washington's Birthday celebration, Sheriff Sánchez had received the good news that outgoing President William Howard Taft had pardoned him for his conviction of violating the Neutrality Laws. It is an interesting quirk of politics that Sheriff Sánchez, a Democrat, was a recipient of the largesse of a presidential pardon handed out by a departing Republican president. The sheriff's former coconspirator, General Bernardo Reyes, was not so fortunate. He was killed leading an attack on the presidential palace in Mexico City twelve days earlier, on February 9 (Cumberland 235).

If justice delayed is justice denied, then the two postponements of the trials of Alonzo W. Allee for the murders of Francisco and Manuel Gutiérrez would prove to be "so great a prejudice" to the victims that by the time the case came up again, the indignation that had followed the homicides would have been overshadowed by the other dramatic deaths and violent events that were becoming commonplace on the border.

Part IV

A JURY OF HIS PEERS

The case of the State of Texas versus Alonzo W. Allee opened on a familiar refrain. It was Monday, May 5, 1913, when the case was called, only to be immediately continued, pending the arrival of a material witness. Once more, as in the previous January, Marshall Hicks claimed to be awaiting the arrival of an important witness and asked for a delay until two o'clock that afternoon, by which time the witness was expected to have arrived on the I&GN train that reached Laredo from San Antonio—and points north—at five minutes till one.

It had been almost four months since the Allee case had been in the news, and a sign that even the newspaper had forgotten a great deal of its history was the headline in the *Laredo Daily Times* of May 5, which read: ABSENT WITNESS CAUSED POSTPONEMENT OF TRIAL FOR KILLING OF FRANCISCO GUTIERREZ SEVERAL HOURS. The *Times* had forgotten that Marshall Hicks, the defense counsel, had announced the previous December that the case of the killing of Manuel Gutiérrez would be tried first.

On May 6 the *Daily Times* reported that the case had been continued until Thursday, May 8, by which time Dr. H. W. A. Lee, the defense witness who was traveling to Laredo from New Orleans, was to have arrived. No more details were given as to who Dr. Lee was or what he was to testify about.

On Thursday, May 8, both sides finally announced that they were ready to go to trial, and "the calling of the veniremen [was] taken up," according to the newspaper. This was the special venire which Article 643 of the *Texas Penal Code* (1893) required in capital cases where there was the possibility of the death penalty being imposed. Judge Mullally had

had one hundred special veniremen summoned, and, according to Article 655 of the *Penal Code* of 1893, each one's name was called "at the court house door." When this was done, it was discovered that twenty-eight of those called had failed to appear, "whereupon a fine of $20 each was imposed on the absentees and they were ordered summoned to appear at once," according to the *Laredo Daily Times* of May 8. Only five jurors were picked that day from the first venire of one hundred men, and another venire of seventy-five was called for the following morning at nine o'clock.

The 175 potential jurors who were called for the Allee case in May 1913, as well as the two hundred called the previous December, were chosen, according to the provisions of Article 372 of the *Texas Penal Code* of 1893, from a list drawn up by a panel of three jury commissioners appointed each judicial term by the district judge. The jury commission selected both the grand jury and the general jury for each term. Unfortunately, we do not have the names of the persons comprising the jury commission of the Forty-ninth Judicial District during the fall of 1912 or the spring of 1913, but, according to the same Article 372, the jury commissioners had to possess the following qualifications:

1) They shall be intelligent citizens of the county and be able to read and write.
2) They shall be freeholders in the county and qualified jurors in the county.
3) They shall be residents of different portions of the county.
4) They shall have no suit in the district court of such county which requires the intervention of a jury.

It is obvious that the composition of the jury commission had an effect on the composition of the venire, and, in a roundabout way, we can deduce the makeup of the first from the makeup of the latter. Of the two hundred special veniremen summoned in December 1912 (one hundred for each of the two cases against Allee), thirty had Spanish surnames in the venire for cause number 4873, and twenty-six had Spanish surnames in cause number 4874. In May 1913 the special venire called for the Allee murder trial originally contained ninety-eight names (not one hundred as the newspaper reported). By the time the typewritten list of veniremen had been prepared, the number had dwindled to ninety, and of these, twenty, or 22 percent of the total, had Spanish surnames.

The first five jurors were chosen from this lot, and none carried a Spanish surname. The *Laredo Daily Times* of May 8, 1913, identified J. N. Worsham, G. R. Weber, Jesse Hewitt, and T. A. Bunn (the latter name incorrectly given by the newspaper as T. A. Bunce).

At the end of the day, with seven jurors still to go, Judge Mullally ordered that seventy-five more prospective jurors be called for the following day and caused the clerk of the district court, R. V. Martin, to issue an order commanding the sheriff to "take the bodies" of several of the truant veniremen who had failed to appear earlier, including "Geo. R. Weber," whom the newspaper had reported that same day as having already been chosen to serve on the jury. Apparently Weber was selected in absentia, in spite of his reluctance to serve. Another missing venireman ordered attached was R. M. Johnson, who was described as being out of town. Perhaps he returned that very evening, for the next day he was picked to serve on the jury.

Of the second special venire, consisting of seventy-five names, eighteen carried Spanish surnames, which translates into 24 percent of the total. In 1900 the Anglo population of Webb County was one-fourth of the total of 21,851 persons. Assuming that the proportions remained unchanged by 1913, the ratio of Spanish-surnamed prospective jurors in these two special venires was the inverse—more or less—to what existed in the general population. This situation was worse than what had existed with the grand jury that indicted Allee, of which one-third had been Spanish-surnamed.

Even allowing for an increase in the Anglo population between 1900 and 1913, that increase would not have materially changed the respective proportions, which remained relatively constant through the first half of the century. By the 1940s, for example, the population of Laredo had roughly doubled from that of 1900, and yet "[t]he composition of the population in the city [showed] that seventy percent of the population [was] Latin American" (Da Camara 3). The *New Handbook of Texas* reports that in 1990 persons of Hispanic descent accounted for 93.9 percent of the Webb County population (6:866). Generally, the trend throughout the twentieth century showed an increase in the population growth of Hispanics in Webb County.

However, in comparing the two ethnic groups—Anglos and Hispanics—in early twentieth-century Webb County, we must, of course, bear in mind that a larger proportion of the Anglos would have been qualified to serve as jurors than would have been the case with Hispanics. Article 687 of the *Texas Code of Criminal Procedure* (1911) provided that in order to serve as a juror a person (male) had to be a "qualified voter" in the county in question and in the state of Texas. A "qualified voter," in turn, had been defined in the Texas case of *Abrigo v. State,* 29th Tex.Ct.App.R. 143 (1890), as one who was a citizen of the state and of the county, a citizen being

> a person, native or naturalized, who has the privilege of voting for public officers, and who is qualified to fill an elective office [this explains why it was said that Sheriff Amador Sánchez had lost his citizenship] . . . may be a foreigner not yet naturalized, but intending to be. . . . The court holds that if the intention to become a citizen has been declared in due form, and the other conditions . . . are found to exist, the individual thereby becomes both a qualified elector and a citizen qualified for jury service. (144)

A prospective juror, in addition to being a qualified voter in the county and the state, was required by Article 687 to answer a second question in the affirmative. The question was: "Are you a householder or a freeholder in the state?" A "householder" was defined by the statute as "He who is the head of and provider of a family occupying a house, whether married or single." A "freeholder" was a property owner. Article 687 (2) also provided that failure to pay poll tax would not disqualify an otherwise qualified voter from serving on a jury.

It would be safe to assume that most, if not all, of the Anglos in Webb County were native-born citizens of the United States and that if they met the state and county residence requirements (one year and six months, respectively), they would have been qualified voters. Of course, if they were not householders or freeholders in the state, they may still not have been qualified jurors. On the other hand, it would also be safe to assume that many of the Hispanics in Webb County were neither citizens nor voters, although they may have been freeholders, as was the case with Manuel Gutiérrez and with his uncle, Julián. This situation would have precluded many Hispanic residents of Webb County from serving on a jury, as would their inability to read or write English. The latter was cause for disqualification under Article 692 (14) of the same 1911 *Code of Criminal Procedure.* Another factor that cannot be discounted is the probability that many of the Hispanics born in the United

States, native-born citizens, would still have been disqualified from jury service for not being freeholders or householders. Still, after taking all these elements into account, the results of the jury selection in the case against Alonzo W. Allee were, nonetheless, remarkable.

Of the eighteen Spanish-surnamed veniremen who presented themselves in district court on Friday, May 9, 1913, not one was selected. Next to the names of the veniremen someone—probably the clerk of the court—often made some abbreviated notations. Some of these are legible and decipherable; others are not. For example, on the second list we find the name "Ed Sanchez" as vireman number 4. A notation of "P" is made to the left, indicating that he was present in court. The abbreviation "Dis" indicates that he was dismissed, but no reason is given for the action. José Treviño, J. F. Herrera, A. F. Peña, and Darío Sánchez were likewise present and were also dismissed. Darío Sánchez certainly met all the requirements of citizenship, having served as alderman of Laredo in the 1870s and twice as mayor in the 1880s, as well as Webb County sheriff, but perhaps his age excused him from jury service (Calderón 1025–1026). P. N. García was present and has a checkmark next to his name, indicating that he was eligible, but his name also appears on the list "Challenges by Defendant," meaning that he was rejected by the defense. Of the eleven prospective jurors rejected by the defense under the right to peremptory challenge, seven had Spanish surnames. Under these conditions, the composition of the jury was a foregone conclusion.

On May 9, 1913, the *Laredo Daily Times* published the list of jurors that would try Alonzo W. Allee for the murder of Manuel Gutiérrez: "The completed jury is as follows, the last seven having been secured from the second special venire of 75 who appeared this morning: Gus Schmitt, J. N. Worsham, G. R. Weber, Jesse Hewitt, T. A. Bunn, R. M. Johnson, G. M. Campbell, R. P. Woodward, J. C. Chamberlain, Sam Mackin, R. S. Dixon and J. W. Brewster."

The composition of this jury was sufficiently skewed that it was bound to raise quite a few eyebrows, as well as provoke unfavorable comment among the Hispanic community. It was left to Justo S. Penn, the editor and publisher of the *Daily Times*, to try to explain the reason for this outcome to the majority of the population in Webb County. Penn found it necessary to add this justification to the news story: "Literally speaking, the jury comprises an all-American panel, which means that the defendant will be tried by a jury of his peers."

Perhaps Penn did not realize the full implications of such a rationale. Under that logic a Mexican defendant would be entitled to be tried by an all-Mexican jury. As an aside, we might mention here that, at the time of the events narrated, the term "Mexican" was generally in use among Anglos to describe not only Mexican citizens but also those persons born in the United States of Mexican descent and that the term encompassed nationality, ethnicity, and race. The historian Roberto Calderón cites an example of this usage when he quotes from the *Galveston News* in 1890: "The population of Laredo is placed at 11,600, three fourths of whom are Mexicans" (857). Fortunately for the Anglo judicial establishment, no Mexican or African American had yet dared to demand to be tried exclusively by Mexican or African American juries. And one wonders how a woman's demand to be tried by a jury composed only of women would have been met, since women were excluded from juries. Nevertheless, that was the spin (to use today's phrase) that Penn had decided to put on the lopsided results of the Allee jury selection.

Actually, in focusing on the importance for a defendant to be tried by a jury of his peers, Penn and Marshall Hicks, who undoubtedly charted the public relations as well as the judicial campaign, were not only following hallowed Anglo-American jurisprudence, they were also anticipating (albeit unintentionally) by some forty years a seminal decision of the United States Supreme Court.

In 1954 the United States Supreme Court decided the case of *Hernandez v. State of Texas*, 347 U.S. 667 (1954). In that case a murder defendant had moved to quash the indictment and the petit jury panel, based on a showing that "persons of Mexican descent were systematically excluded from service of jury commissioners, grand jurors, and petit jurors, although they were qualified to serve." Hernández lost at both the trial court and before the Texas Court of Criminal Appeals, but the United States Supreme Court reversed those judgments, holding:

> [I]t is a denial of the equal protection of the laws to try a defendant of a particular race or color under an indictment issued by a grand jury, or before a petit jury from which all persons of his race or color have, solely because of that race or color, been excluded by the State, whether acting through its legislature, its courts, or its executive or administrative offices [footnote omitted]. (670)

Marshall Hicks, speaking through the editor of the *Laredo Daily Times*, turned the rationale for *Hernandez* and similar cases on its head forty-one years before *Hernandez* was decided. In the State of Texas versus Alonzo W. Allee, it was determined by the defense, with the acquiescence of the prosecution, that it was not enough to avoid excluding jurors of the same ethnic group or race as the defendant. Instead, it was imperative that all the jurors belong to the same ethnic group or race as the defendant—as long as the defendant was an Anglo.

We know why Marshall Hicks would embrace such a proposition, but it is more difficult to understand why Justo S. Penn would allow himself to be made the spokesman for the defense. The facile explanation would be Penn's ongoing association with Hicks through the Democratic Party, but Justo S. Penn was too complex a man for this to be the only answer. The key to Penn's character can probably be found in the name he chose for himself: *Justo Sabor* Penn. He was born in Austin, Texas, on October 4, 1875, to James Saunders Penn, brother-in-law to John Ireland, Governor of Texas from 1883 to 1887, and to Virginia Josephine Muller, neither of whom was likely to have given him the name "Justo Sabor" at his christening.

James Saunders Penn (the elder) moved his printing business from Austin to Laredo in May 1881, so that by the time the Texas-Mexican and the International and Great Northern Railroads reached Laredo in the fall, Penn had already been publishing the *Laredo Times* for several months. By most accounts James Saunders Penn was a crusading editor, railing against corruption and unsanitary conditions in his adopted city. He also dabbled unsuccessfully in local politics, running in November 1886 for state representative and losing "by less than fifty votes in a heated and apparently fraudulent election" (Calderón 791). In 1887, according to the *New Handbook of Texas*, Penn was confined to a mental institution in Austin. Penn later returned to Laredo and to running the newspaper, but he suffered a relapse in 1901 and was again confined to the asylum. After a brief stay there he was released, and again he returned to Laredo. However, after his return home he committed suicide on May 17, 1901, after he had shot and killed a friend (Cearly 5:139).

His son, James Saunders Penn Jr., a.k.a. Justo Sabor Penn, who a short time before had been serving in the Spanish-American War, took over the *Laredo Daily Times* after his father's death. He was not yet twenty-six years of age. A scant four months after his father's death,

Justo married Alicia Herrera, and in doing so became one of the "Mexicanized" Anglos who are described by Gilberto Miguel Hinojosa in his book about Laredo, *A Borderlands Town in Transition:*

> In the process of rapid growth [during the late nineteenth century] Laredo developed into two societies, one Anglo-American and one Mexican-American. The Anglo-American was depicted in the pages of the *Laredo Times.* Founded in 1881, the *Times* boasted of the town's energetic growth, reported the activities of the various social clubs and church-related schools and kept Laredoans abreast of state and national news. . . . Anglo-Americans could not remain completely apart, however, and some limited social mixing and intermarriage did take place among the upper classes. . . . According to local tradition, from this and from daily interaction with the large Mexican population, some Anglos became Mexicanized.   (119–120)

Somewhere along the way, probably during his days in the Laredo public schools, James Saunders Jr. had acquired his new name. We know that young Penn had attended Southwestern University in Georgetown, Texas, in 1891 and 1892, when he was sixteen and seventeen, and that while at Southwestern Penn was already matriculated as "Justo S. Penn." A plausible scenario for the renaming of young Penn might have included a Laredo wit who, noticing the propensity at that time for Anglo men to use only the initials of their given names, would have found it amusing to supply "Justo Sabor" for "J. S." "Justo Sabor," the right (or just) taste (or flavor), calls to mind an advertising slogan, perhaps for some beverage. The first part of the name, "Justo," would have appealed to the young man who later, as a journalist, strove to bring justice through his editorials, such as in his condemnation of the assassination of President Madero.

James Saunders Penn Jr. became Justo S. Penn and, in the process, he transformed himself from one of those Anglo newcomers who had followed the railroads to Laredo into a native son. He had been brought to Laredo when he was only a child of five. The *Laredo Times,* in a special centennial edition of June 13, 1981, related that within days of the family's arrival in Laredo a daughter was born to the Penns, whom the parents named Bonita. The choice of "Bonita," meaning "pretty" in Spanish, may have signaled the family's willingness to embrace the new culture in which they now found themselves, but in any case the word is close to "bonny" in both sound and meaning, a term which they would have found pleasing.

The young Justo would have taken the gesture to heart, later assimilating himself to a considerable extent into the Hispanic culture and even marrying into it. No doubt he saw himself as syncretizing the distinctive elements of his hometown—the Anglo and the Hispanic cultures, as well as the interests of the old Anglo ranchers who had intermarried with the old Mexican landed families and of the newcomers concerned primarily with commerce, farming, and land development.

But Justo S. Penn, the mediator and synthesizer, was also the nephew of a former Democratic governor of Texas, John Ireland. Penn himself had been elected in 1910 as a Democrat to a term in the Texas Legislature and served as chairman of the Democratic Executive Committee of Webb County until 1926, according to the *New Handbook of Texas* (Young, "Penn," 5:139). The mediator could clearly also be partisan. When it came time to help political friends such as Marshall Hicks, Penn did so, although it must have been difficult for him to sell the community on the course that justice seemed to be taking with the Allee trial.

After attempting to justify the composition of the Allee jury, Penn then published the names of the jurors, without giving any particulars about any of them. Perhaps additional information was not necessary because the paper's readers were already acquainted with them, or perhaps it was thought wiser not to do so. Some of those jurors were sufficiently prominent, however, that publications of the time that still survive occasionally have information about them. For example, J. N. Worsham, who was chosen foreman of the jury, had his photograph in Falvella's *Souvenir Album of Laredo*, on page 10, in a group portrait of federal officials, where he was identified as the postmaster.

Sam Mackin was also featured by Falvella in a group labeled "Some of the Prominent Business Men of Laredo," on page 13, and identified later, on page 37, as "manager Laredo Water Co. and Consumers Ice & Fuel Co." Mackin had been born in Ohio in 1867 and moved to Texas with his family in 1878. He came to Laredo in 1892 to take charge of the water and ice plant at Fort McIntosh, an experience that served him well when he made his transition to the private sector (Green, *Border Biographies* [2:72–73]).

Another prominent business man, although not listed by Falvella, was T. A. Bunn. Bunn's biography is also included in Green's *Border Biographies* (taken from the *New Encyclopedia of Texas,* published in 1929). T. A. Bunn—no given names—is described as having been born in Jackson County, Alabama, in 1862, which made him fifty-one at the time of the Allee trial. He had been a passenger conductor on the International & Great Northern Railroad while living in San Antonio, from 1883 to 1893. In 1893 he went to Mexico to take a position with the Mexican National Railroad and stayed there until 1912. The outbreak of the Mexican Revolution in 1910 ended his railroad career, and he moved to Laredo (presumably by early 1912, or he would not have met the residency requirements to qualify as a juror), where he seems to have immediately become successful in developing residential real estate. His biographer stated respectfully: "Mr. Bunn is the man who made Heights District in Laredo, having bought this section and developed it, until it is now [1929] one of the finest residential sections of Laredo" (2:15–16). The Heights District had been developed as the Anglo quarter of Laredo, but its founding antedated Bunn's arrival, the land in question having been part of the incentives granted by the City of Laredo to the investors of the Texas-Mexican Railroad in the 1880s (Calderón 577–579).

T. A. Bunn apparently had a brother in Laredo, also a successful businessman and also born in Jackson County, Alabama. His name was Woodie Y. Bunn and he owned the Laredo Creamery Company. Woodie Y. Bunn was undoubtedly the same "W. Y. Bunn" who had signed an affidavit the previous January, claiming that "so great a prejudice" existed in Webb County against Alonzo W. Allee that he could not receive a fair trial, thereby supporting Allee's motion for a change of venue.

Another juror, J. C. Chamberlain, may have been related to William Chapman Chamberlain, whose prominence lay in part in his family connections with Captain Richard King, a brother-in-law. Another juror, G. R. Weber, was presumably the same as George Weber, who is listed in the 1910 census of Webb County as a twenty-seven-year-old telegraph or telephone manager—the words are almost illegible. Weber had been born in Texas, but his parents came from Germany. Still another juror, R. M. Johnson, was described in the 1910 census as a "laborer" and was then (in 1910) thirty-seven years old, a native of Arkansas.

Not enough is known about the men who comprised the jury that was to judge Alonzo Allee's guilt or innocence, but from the scant details we have it appears that many, if not most, were not native Texans, certainly not native Laredoans. They were probably more representative of the Anglo newcomers to Webb County, the settlers who came with or after the railroads to engage in business or commercial farming, than of the early Anglo settlers who had intermarried with the locals and gravitated toward ranching. As a consequence, the latecomers were less sympathetic to the Hispanic population of the area. David Montejano, in *Anglos and Mexicans in the Making of Texas, 1836–1986*, describes the exacerbation of ethnic tensions that occurred around 1900 between the old-timers and the newcomers and the reasons behind it:

> The farm colonies recruited by ranchers and developers made their presence felt throughout the Southwest, and nearly everywhere one can find incidents and episodes of tension between old and new residents. While this meeting between cowboys and farmers played itself out throughout the state, nowhere did it reverberate with such dramatic and explosive force as among the Mexican settlements of the border region. . . .
>
> In the context of the Texas border, this transformation assumed a sharp racial character with generally tragic consequences. . . . It undermined the accommodative "peace structure," which for two generations had contained the sentiments and politics of race antagonism. Thus, this conflict represented much more than just a rancher-farmer confrontation. It was a conflict between two distinct societies. (104)

With the jury seated, the case of the State of Texas versus Alonzo W. Allee was finally ready to commence. The trial began with a plea of not guilty from the defendant. On Friday, May 9, 1913, the *Laredo Daily Times* informed the readers who were getting ready to peruse its pages after supper: "The taking of evidence will begin this afternoon and it is probable that this feature alone will consume all the afternoon and a large portion of tomorrow and the case will not go to the jury until Monday at the earliest."

The state, having the burden of proof, would present its evidence first in an attempt to prove that Alonzo W. Allee did, indeed, "with malice aforethought kill Manuel Gutierrez Garcia by shooting him with a gun," as the indictment alleged. The state called sixteen witnesses. The first two were Laureano Gutiérrez and his brother, Francisco Gutiérrez, cousins of the deceased, whose testimony as to the occurrences at La Volanta was first taken by Justice of the Peace Nicasio Idar. The next witness was their father, Julián Gutiérrez, and his statement had also been first taken by Idar. Laureano, of course, had been the only eyewitness to the killing of Manuel Gutiérrez.

Three other witnesses could be said to be from the law enforcement side. They were Nicasio Idar, who had conducted the first investigation of the killings at the scene of the crime, and Willie Stoner and Sam McKenzie, the deputy sheriffs who had accompanied Idar to La Volanta (or "El Alamito," as the newspapers referred to the ranch). Stoner and McKenzie could be expected to testify as to the results of their investigation, if any, and perhaps add to Idar's description of the location but not to the arrest of the defendant. Allee had turned himself in to Deputy Sheriff J. E. Hill at Webb, Texas, but Hill was not called as a witness by the state. Hill's absence from the roster of the state's witnesses is remarkable, because he would have been able to testify as to what Allee had done and said when he turned himself in. Of course, Hill had been on the grand jury that indicted Allee—another odd feature of this case.

Three of the state's witnesses were family members of the deceased. Two of these were the widows, identified as Mrs. Manuel Gutiérrez and Mrs. Francisco Gutiérrez. Francisca and Manuela could only have testified about what they knew firsthand, for example, the reason for their husbands' visit to La Volanta, or perhaps their observations of the state of mind of the two men when they set out to meet with Allee. They could have also testified, of course, about Manuel's good qualities as husband, father, and son in order to elicit sympathy for the victim from the jury. They might have even been asked if Manuel had had a violent temper or if he had been involved in altercations before. Unfortunately, none of the women's testimony was preserved or reported in the newspaper.

The third family member to testify was Manuel Gutiérrez's brother-in-law, Ernesto Flores, who had forwarded the lease payment from Alonzo Allee to Manuel. Originally, Ernesto Flores had also been scheduled as a defense witness, but his name was crossed out on this list. Flores's testimony would have been limited to his part as an intermediary in the transaction. Along with this testimony the state introduced the check for $450.26, drawn on the Stockman's National Bank of Cotulla, from Alonzo W. Allee to Manuel Gutiérrez or "Bearer." The envelope in which Flores had forwarded the check to Manuel Gutiérrez was also made part of the record.

Five of the state's witnesses likewise appeared on the defense's list. Two of these were Dr. W. E. Lowry, who presumably was to testify as to the cause of death of the victim, and the elusive Pedro Medrano, who is identified only as a resident of Webb County, where he was subpoenaed by the defense. The 1910 census of Webb County contains only one Medrano family. It was the family of Atanacio Medrano, thirty-three years of age, who lived at 1213 Coke Street. Atanacio Medrano is identified as a "laborer" who did "odd jobs." He was married and had four children, the eldest of whom was ten-year-old Pedro. This bit of information raises more questions than it answers. Was this Pedro, who would have been twelve in 1912, one and the same as the important material witness for whom the trial had been postponed? Of course, that witness had been originally reported by the newspaper as being named Ramón Medrano, and we never learned whether Ramón and Pedro were the same person.

Two other joint witnesses were Deputy Sheriff Sam McKenzie and Deputy Sheriff Willie Stoner, previously mentioned. The name of Frank Dillard also appeared on both lists of witnesses, but again there is no record of his testimony. The only information we have of a Frank Dillard comes from the 1910 census, in which he is listed as the son of John Dillard, a sixty-one-year-old "stockman." Frank was twenty-four at the time, a "ranchman," single, living in his father's household, which was located in the rural part of the county. Frank may have been a ranch hand of Allee's or a neighbor, but we have no indication as to the reason why his testimony was deemed necessary by both parts.

The remaining state's witnesses were Antonio Salinas, Eusebio García, Ygnacio Benavides, A. M. Bruni, the Webb County treasurer, and Macedonio Guerra.

The state began the presentation of its case on the afternoon of Friday, May 9, at which time an unsigned witness attachment order was issued to compel the presence in court of "N. Idar, Dr. W. E. Lowry, A. M. Bruni, Eusebio García, Ygnacio Benavides, and Macedonio Guerra." Article 523 of the *Texas Penal Code* of 1893 provided for a writ of attachment in any criminal action, "commanding some peace officer to take the body of a witness and bring him before [the court] to testify in behalf of the state or of the defendant, as the case may be." A writ of attachment would normally be issued after a subpoena—that is, a summons—had failed to secure the presence and testimony of the witness, as provided by Article 524 of the *Texas Penal Code* of 1893:

When a witness who resides in the county of the prosecution has been duly served with a subpoena to appear and testify in any criminal action or proceeding fails to so appear, the state or the defendant shall be entitled to have an attachment issued forthwith for such witness.

It is possible that after the previous postponements of the Allee trial some of the witnesses—particularly those like Nicasio Idar and Dr. W. E. Lowry, who would be the most likely to have pressing business to attend to—might not have felt the necessity of presenting themselves in court until they were certain that the trial had indeed begun. Deputy Sheriff Stoner did "take the bodies" of Idar, Lowry, Benavides, and Guerra. A. M. Bruni and Eusebio García had a notation by their names, indicating that they were out of the city or out of the county— the last word is not completely legible. However, the final list of the state's witnesses shows an "A" (for absent) notation by the names of Eusebio García, Ygnacio Benavides, A. M. Bruni, and Macedonio Guerra. These four could not be found— or did not want to be found—although A. M. Bruni, as county treasurer, should have been easy to locate. All in all, it seemed as if the prosecution was having a difficult time convincing—or compelling—many of its witnesses to testify.

On Saturday, May 10, the *Laredo Daily Times* reported that "[d]uring the progress of the Allee trial yesterday afternoon the time was consumed in the introduction of evidence by the state, who also continued to introduce testimony up to this forenoon, when they rested."

The following day, May 11, was a Sunday, so there was no activity in court, and the trial did not resume until Monday, May 12. Since the state concluded the presentation of its case on Saturday morning, the *Laredo Daily Times* reported that same evening, May 10, "just before noon the first witness for the defense testified."

The state had scheduled seventeen witnesses for its case but probably called only twelve. Marshall Hicks, for the defense, listed fifty-five witnesses, although not all were called. Hicks had cast his net for witnesses far and wide and apparently without consideration of expense or trouble. Dr. H. W. A. Lee, for example, was brought from New Orleans, and the trial had been delayed by three days awaiting his arrival. We do not know what Dr. Lee's testimony consisted of, but it is probable that he was called as an expert witness in forensic medicine. Other witnesses were not so exalted. One was Juan Cruz, residing (according to the subpoena application) at 214 South Colorado Street in San Antonio, Bexar County, Texas. Juan Cruz's "avocation" was given as "peddlar" in the subpoena application, which was actually signed by Geo. M. Martin, "of counsel for A. W. Allee, the defendant," and not by Hicks.

Other witnesses subpoenaed at the same time were A. P. Oliver of Floresville, in Wilson County, identified as "Saloon Prop."; M. L. Crass (or Cross), a stockman of Frio County; Wm. Stanush, a county commissioner of Atascosa County; and John Winn, the sheriff of Atascosa County. The last two, however, do not appear on the final list of defendant's witnesses, nor do two other residents of Atascosa County also listed, a liveryman and a justice of the peace.

What the purpose was for calling up these witnesses can only be guessed at. Perhaps they were meant to be character witnesses from the various parts of the state where Allee had had contacts before. If so, his experiences in Atascosa County must not have been very edifying, since none of the witnesses from there were called. On the other hand, perhaps the reason for subpoenaing such a wide and diverse array of potential witnesses was in the nature of a preventive measure to find out negative aspects of Allee's life and sanitize them before the prosecution could make use of them. They need not have worried.

The defense witnesses actually called were probably limited only to those with some type of notation (such as an "S" for served or a checkmark) by their names. These were Dr. W. E. Lowry, Frank Dillard, Pedro Medrano, A. J. Landrum (the lessee of La Volanta), M. D. DeSpain (a "stockman," according to the 1910 census), Sam Yates, W. H. Hobbs, R. A. Carr, T. A. Coleman, Dr. H. W. A. Lee, H. C. Johnson, S. V. Edwards, Willie Stoner, Sam Mckenzie, and the defendant himself, Alonzo W. Allee.

Willie Stoner and Sam McKenzie—or "McKinzie," "McKinsey," as it was sometimes spelled—were, of course, the two deputy sheriffs who had accompanied Nicasio Idar to La Volanta to investigate the crimes. Sam McKenzie appears—as McKinzie—in a 1911 photograph of Texas Rangers in Laredo (Schreiner 95). Alonzo Allee's son, Ranger captain A. Y. Allee, had mentioned Sam "Mckenzie" as one of the Rangers who would visit his father's ranch (Pattie, "A. Y. Allee" 43). Sam "McKinzie" was also the hangman who, on March 15, 1912, had executed J. B. Compton for the murder of Levytansky, the Laredo jeweler, according to the district court minutes signed by him: "[Compton] was executed by me on Friday the 15th March 1912. . . . Hanged within the walls of the County jail by then and there hanging J. B. Compton by the neck until he was dead [signed: Sam McKinsey]" (Worley 27).

Except for Dr. Lee, who had traveled from New Orleans to testify, the defense witnesses were all from Texas, although not all were from Webb County. Again, the question arises: how would the testimony of these witnesses from outside the county contribute to elucidating the matter under investigation—the killing of Manuel Gutiérrez? W. H. Hobbs, for example, lived in San Antonio, according to the application for subpoena filed by Marshall Hicks, so unless he was to testify as to Allee's character or had been brought as some kind of expert witness, there was little that Hobbs could have added to the inquiry. This was particularly true in light of the theory on which Hicks had determined to base his defense, one that had worked well for Alonzo Allee's father: self-defense or justifiable homicide.

The Texas law of justifiable homicide was a most forgiving one. As late as 1942 a commentator writing for the *Texas Law Review* had this to say about justifiable homicide in this state:

> Justification as bar to conviction of a defendant who is prose-
> cuted on a charge of unlawful homicide covers a greater variety
> of specific types of defenses in Texas than at English common
> law. In addition, in some of the instances where the excuses
> under Texas law are generally the same as at common law, their
> operative scope is in Texas much more favorable to the accused
> than it is elsewhere.   (STUMBERG 17)

Chapter Twelve of the *Texas Penal Code* of 1911 was devoted to justifiable homicide. Article 1087 of the same chapter provided that "[h]omicide is justifiable in the cases enumerated in the succeeding articles of this chapter" and proceeded to so enumerate, beginning with Article 1088, which dealt with killing of a public enemy:

> It is lawful to kill a public enemy, not only in the prosecution of
> war, but when he may be in the act of hostile invasion or occu-
> pation of any part of the state. . . . Persons belonging to hostile
> tribes of Indians who habitually commit depradations upon the
> lives or property of inhabitants of this state, and all persons act-
> ing with such tribes are public enemies, and this whether found

in the act of committing such depradations or under circumstances which sufficiently show an intention to do so.

The next article, 1089, added the following caption: "But not by poison." Homicide of a public enemy by poison "or the use of poisoned weapons" was not justifiable. The lawmakers obviously felt that a sense of fair play must be maintained, even in dealing with public enemies.

The list continued with other instances of homicide which were also deemed justified and which are still recognized today, such as the execution of convicts found guilty of capital offenses and the killing by a law officer of a person resisting arrest.

Part Four of Chapter Twelve of the 1911 code dealt with justifiable homicide "in defense of person or property." Article 1105 of the *Penal Code* of 1911 recited:

> Homicide is permitted by law when inflicted for the purpose of preventing the offense of murder, rape, robbery, maiming, disfiguring, castration, arson, burglary and theft at night, or when inflicted upon a person or persons who are found armed with deadly weapons and in disguise in the night time on premises not his or their own, whether the homicide be committed by the party about to be injured or by some person in his behalf, when the killing takes place under the following circumstances:

There followed nine separate conditions under which the homicide would be found justifiable. The first of these conditions provided a most elastic justification. It read: "It must reasonably appear by the acts or by words, coupled with the acts of the person killed, that it was the purpose and intent of such person to commit one of the offenses above named."

Case law dating back to the nineteenth century firmly established the doctrine contained in the statute that placed perception or apprehension above reality. In *Munden v. State,* a Texas Supreme Court case from 1873, the court held that "[i]t is sufficient that a reasonable man should have ground to apprehend or fear the danger, in order to justify his using force to repel it" (*Reports of Cases Argued and Decided in the Supreme Court of the State of Texas, 1874,* 353–354).

As justifiable homicide, then, was how the defense depicted its version of the double killings of Francisco and Manuel Gutiérrez. It is what is known as an affirmative defense, where the defendant says: "I did it, but it is not a crime because . . ." and gives an excuse or justification that is recognized by the law. The defendant has the burden of proving its contention when pleading an affirmative defense. In this case, Marshall Hicks, or the defense, had the burden of pleading justifiable homicide and of producing sufficient evidence of it to persuade the jury to acquit. In order to meet all these burdens—pleading, production, and persuasion—Hicks would have been obliged to put his client on the stand to tell the jury his side of the story, and he did.

At the conclusion of the presentation of the evidence by both sides, the jury would have heard two versions of the events of August 14, 1912: the testimony of Laureano Gutiérrez as to what he had seen and heard that day at La Volanta and Alonzo Allee's story. It only remained for counsel for each side to try to make the jury believe its version of the facts. One interesting fact garnered from the story in the *Laredo Daily Times* of Monday, May 12, was the mention that A. C. Hamilton had given the final argument for the prosecution and had concluded his talk at noon.

Where was District Attorney John Anthony Valls at this crucial part of the trial? Why did he allow his second chair and former political rival, A. C. Hamilton, to hold the spotlight when it came to giving the closing argument? Valls was the silver-tongued orator who never missed an opportunity to speak, according to his biographer and other sources:

> Valls, however, was not only an able prosecuting attorney, but an excellent orator as well. From a newspaper [*Laredo Times*, June 14, 1916] was found the following:
> "Hon. John A. Valls was chosen to orate on A Flag Day Exercise held at the Elks Hall last night.
> "The oration of the evening, 'Patriotism,' by Hon. John A. Valls was one of the most eloquent and inspiring talks ever made in this city on a similar subject. . . . As District Attorney he has been heard by many, but last night, as orator of the evening at the Elks Flag Day exercises, Mr. Valls held the audience spellbound." (WORLEY 30)

And in 1935, in a talk given by Yale Hicks, Marshall Hicks's brother and law partner, titled "History of the Webb County Bench and Bar," Yale Hicks made reference to Valls, saying that he was "noted for his unusual ability as a prosecutor and for his upright character as a lawyer and his brilliance as an orator" (Green, *John Valls* 13).

John Anthony Valls was probably not in court as A. C. Hamilton made his arguments to the jury.

One curious fact mentioned in the newspaper story of May 12 was about a stipulation that both sides had entered into: "The defense closed by reading an agreement which they had reached with the state regarding the weight and height of the defendant." Neither height nor weight were given in the story, though. A subsequent description of Alonzo W. Allee gave his height as five feet and nine and three-quarters inches, although his weight does not appear. The purpose of this stipulation could only have had the purpose of comparing Allee's size with that of his victims, perhaps to show that Francisco and Manuel Gutiérrez had been taller and heavier than Allee.

Once the lawyers were finished with their arguments to the jury, it was up to the judge to address the jury, charging them with the law which they were supposed to apply in relation to the evidence that had been put before them. Up till then Judge Mullally would have remained a more or less silent referee, ruling only when called to do so by the parties on various points of evidence. Now it was the judge's turn to hold the center of the stage, but only within the well-defined parameters allowed him by law. Texans did not want their judges to wield too much power, as illustrated by Article 715 of the *Texas Penal Code* of 1893:

> After the argument of any criminal cause has been concluded,
> the judge shall deliver to the jury a written charge, in which
> he shall distinctly set forth the law applicable to the case; but he
> shall not express any opinion as to the weight of evidence, nor
> shall he sum up testimony.

This limitation must have accorded well with Judge Mullally's view of his role. In his 1916 *Souvenir Album of Laredo*, Falvella had been fulsome in his praise of District Judge John F. Mullally. However, Mullally must have been a less colorful character than his political comrade-in-arms and fellow Republican, the district attorney, because much less has been written about the judge despite his long tenure on the bench. The Webb County census of 1900 lists John Francis Mullally as a forty-two-year-old lawyer who was born in Illinois of parents born in Ireland. He had been appointed to the bench of the Forty-ninth Judicial District of Texas in 1905, according to Seb Wilcox, as related by Lott and Martínez in *The Kingdom of Zapata* (168). Yale Hicks, Marshall's brother, also recalled that Judge John F. Mullally had been appointed "by Governor Lanham. . . . He was confirmed by the State Senate, being enthusiastically supported by Honorable Marshall Hicks, who at that time was a member of the Texas Senate" (Green, *John Valls* 10–11). A photograph shows Mullally, probably in his seventies (he was fifty-five in 1913), with a ferocious white mustache, wire-rimmed eyeglasses, and the stern expression of a "hanging judge." There is no evidence that he was that, with the exception of the Compton case and perhaps others we do not know about.

Judge Mullally's written instructions to the Allee jury covered eleven pages. Of course, a judge does not invent the wheel every time he instructs the jury as to the law of a case. There are forms, as a law professor once advised his class. In 1913 there were forms, too, with blank spaces provided to fill in the names of the defendant and the victim, the name of the county, term of the court, and date of the crime. The form utilized by Judge Mullally in the Allec trial recited the elements of the crime of murder in its various degrees of culpability.

First-degree murder, which was a capital offense, carried a punishment of death or life imprisonment. In order to find a defendant guilty of first-degree murder, the jury was obligated to make a finding of express malice in the defendant's actions. Express malice was defined as "where one with sedate, deliberate mind and formed design unlawfully kills another."

Where the jury could not make a determination of express malice but was able to find implied malice, the result would be murder in the second degree. The punishment for second-degree murder was confinement in the penitentiary for a period left to the jury's discretion, provided that it would be for no less than five years. Implied malice was defined as that "which the law infers from or imputes to certain acts, however suddenly done."

Judge Mullally then instructed the jury as to the lesser included offense of manslaughter, defined as "voluntary homicide, committed under the immediate influence of sudden passion, arising from an adequate cause, but neither justified nor excused by law." The jury was also instructed as to what was deemed to be adequate cause, this added in what appears to be the judge's own handwriting (from comparison with his signature). Adequate cause was "an assault and battery by the deceased, causing pain." If the jury found the defendant guilty of manslaughter, then the punishment called for was confinement in the state penitentiary for any term of "not less than two nor more than five years."

Finally, the standard jury charge provided for a finding of killing in self-defense, in which case the jury should acquit the defendant. The form instructions read:

> A reasonable apprehension of death or great bodily harm will excuse a party in using all necessary force to protect his life or person, and it is *not necessary that there should be actual danger* provided he acted upon a reasonable apprehension of danger as it appeared to him from his standpoint at the time, and in such case the party acting under such real or apparent danger *is in no event bound to retreat in order to avoid the necessity of killing* his assailant [emphasis added].

The frontier mentality was certainly alive and well in this provision. A man was not required to "retreat farther than the air at his back," as the popular saying went, to avoid danger to himself—or killing another. The judge's instructions continued, further defining killing in self-defense:

> If from the evidence you believe the defendant killed the said Manuel Gutierrez Garcia but further believe that at the time of so doing the deceased *or the deceased and Francisco Gutierrez Garza* [the underscored phrases were inserted, handwritten, between the lines] had made an attack on him which, from the manner and character of it and the relative strength of the parties and the defendant's knowledge of the character and disposition of the deceased, caused him to have a reasonable expectation or fear of death or serious bodily injury, and that acting under such reasonable expectation or fear, the defendant killed the deceased, then you should acquit him.

Several aspects of the trial become clear after reviewing the charge on self-defense. For example, the reason for the stipulation as to the defendant's height and weight becomes apparent with the reference to the "relative strength of the parties." The charge, likewise, provides an explanation for the defense calling as witnesses persons who did not have information as to the killings, but who might have testified as to the "character and disposition of the deceased." Neighbors and employees or former employees come to mind in this category.

Sam Yates, for example, was called as a witness by the defense. Yates owned land adjoining Survey 1030, owned by Francisco Gutiérrez Garza in Webb County and included in La Volanta Ranch. Yates was apparently also a neighbor of the Gutiérrez family in Zapata County, owning land or doing business near the San Juan Ranch. When Ernesto Flores had forwarded Allee's lease payment to his brother-in-law, Manuel Gutiérrez, the letter had been addressed to "Señor Manuel Gutiérrez García, c/o Mr. S. A. Yates, Aguilares, Texas."

It seems obvious that the defense had hoped to present the victim in an unfavorable light by introducing testimony which would show that Manuel had a bad temper (we have no indication that this was so) or a bad reputation that would have justified Allee's killing him. We can draw this inference, even without a transcript of the testimony, from the fact that the judge's instructions to the jury raised the issue of the "character and disposition" of the victim. It is, of course, a common defense tactic to put the victim on trial.

Judge Mullally's instructions on self-defense continued:

> [A]nd if the deceased was armed at the time he was killed and was making such attack on defendant, and if the weapon used by him [the deceased] and the manner of its use were such as were reasonably calculated to produce death or serious bodily harm, then the law presumes the deceased intended to murder or aimed to inflict serious bodily injury upon the defendant.

This portion of the charge to the jury explains how Alfred Y. Allee, the defendant's father, was able to be acquitted every time he was tried for murder. In those days when men strapped on a gun whenever they put on their boots, especially when traveling and while in the brush, the first man to draw—and hit the target—won. An armed man was fair game, even if he never drew his weapon, as had been the case with Don Francisco Gutiérrez Garza. Manuel Gutiérrez had allegedly drawn his pistol and fired one shot. However, Laureano Gutiérrez's testimony and Nicasio Idar's observations indicate that if Manuel did fire his pistol, he did so only after Alonzo Allee had already shot him. According to Idar, the victim's bullet had ended "at the feet of Manuel." If

Manuel pulled the trigger, it had been the act of a man already mortally wounded.

Marshall Hicks had tailored the trial very precisely so that his client's actions were covered by the generous blanket of absolution provided by the theory of self-defense. Still, Hicks was not satisfied to simply fall within the parameters of the standard jury instructions. A case can stand or fall on counsel's ability to have his own special instructions given to the jury. Article 717 of the *Penal Code* of 1893 provided for this:

> After or before the charge of the court to the jury the counsel on
> both sides may present written instructions and ask that they
> be given to the jury. The court shall either give or refuse these
> charges, with or without modification, and certify thereto; and
> where the court shall modify a charge it shall be done in writing
> and in such manner as to clearly show what the modification is.

In the Allee case the special instructions are recognizable because they are typed in a different typeface from the standard form. There are three separate instructions and, although they are not identified as to source, a textual analysis of each provides the necessary clues. The first set of special instructions comes on page 6, and its purpose indicates that the provenance was the state. It comes at the end of the charge on second-degree murder. The state clearly did not believe that it could secure a verdict of first-degree murder. Even with Laureano Gutiérrez's testimony, it was not possible to find express malice in Allee's killing of Manuel and Francisco Gutiérrez. Therefore, the state was ostensibly pressing for second-degree murder, claiming that the defendant had

> with a deadly weapon . . . in sudden passion aroused without
> adequate cause and not in defense of himself against an unlawful
> attack, real or apparent . . . and not under circumstances which
> would reduce the offense to the grade of manslaughter, with
> intent to kill, did unlawfully and with implied malice shoot
> and thereby kill said Manuel Gutierrez Garcia.

With these instructions the prosecution was asking for "murder-two" and hoping for manslaughter. The instructions certainly muddied the waters by using terms such as "in sudden passion aroused," which related to manslaughter. Reciting "implied malice" did not undo the damage done by mixing elements of second-degree murder with those of manslaughter. The question that arises is whether this was an instance of deliberate incompetence.

The defense got two sets of instructions to the state's one. The first one came at the end of the charge on self-defense. Marshall Hicks, not content with covering all his bases concerning the defendant's claim that he had acted in self-defense, to protect himself from death or serious bodily harm, now added the claim of defense of property and, more particularly, defense of habitation. Article 1104 of the *Texas Penal Code* of 1911 stated that homicide was permitted "in the necessary defense of person *or property* [emphasis added]." Article 1110 further delineated the circumstances under which homicide in defense of property was justified:

1) The possession [of the property] must be corporeal, and not of a mere right, and the possession must be actual and not merely constructive.
2) The possession must be legal though the right of the property may not be in the possessor.
3) If possession be once lost, it is not lawful to regain it by such means as result in homicide.

Taking the statutes as a point of departure, Hicks had the following special instruction included in the charge to the jury:

So, also, if you believe from the evidence that the defendant had the premises rented, on which the homicide occurred, and if deceased and Francisco Gutierrez Garza were in the act of forcibly ejecting defendant from the house, and defendant to avoid being driven out by force, shot and killed deceased, he was justified in so doing, provided he resorted to all other means to prevent being so driven out before killing, except that he was not bound to retreat in any event.

Marshall Hicks's genius lay in taking a case decision which, on its face, would appear to go against him, and turning it on its head so that it buttressed his own position. In 1910 the Texas Supreme Court decided the case of *Gay v. State*, 125 S.W. 896. In that case Gay, the owner of a house where Gossett lived, was convicted of second-degree murder for killing Gossett, whom he wanted to evict. There was disputed testimony as to whether the deceased had threatened to shoot Gay before Gay shot him. Nevertheless, the jury convicted Gay, and the conviction withstood appeal.

The facts in the *Gay* case were a mirror image of the Allee situation. In *Gay* the landlord had killed the tenant. Here the tenant, Allee, had killed his landlords. But *Gay* raised and answered two important questions. The first related to whether Allee had any right to be on the Gutiérrez lands of La Volanta. The *Gay* opinion made reference to Article 3250 of the *Revised Civil Statutes* of 1895 (Article 5489 of the *Revised Statutes* of 1911) which provided that a tenant was "prohibited from renting or leasing the lands or tenements to another person without obtaining the consent of the landlord" (*Gay* 900). Landrum, the lessee of la Volanta, had clearly not obtained the consent of Don Francisco Gutiérrez before allowing Allee to take possession of the ranch, which would make Allee a trespasser. However, the court in *Gay* found that, even if the deceased was a trespasser, the landlord could not kill the tenant in an attempt to forcibly eject him (900).

Reading this particular special instruction between the lines, we apprehend that Hicks was telling the jury that Francisco and Manuel Gutiérrez had come to La Volanta on August 14, 1912, with the intention of forcibly ejecting Alonzo W. Allee from the premises. That was, undoubtedly, what Allee had testified to. The question that no one seems to have raised was: If Francisco Gutiérrez had intended to evict Allee, why did he go to the trouble of having a new lease drawn up for Allee to sign?

Another issue that emerges from this special instruction is whether Allee was a trespasser at la Volanta under Article 3250, or if he was indeed renting La Volanta, as Hicks wanted the jury to believe. One fact that seems to strengthen Hicks's contention is the lease payment made by Allee to Manuel Gutiérrez. The check, drawn on the Stockmen's National Bank of Cotulla and dated July 6, 1912, was presented for payment on August 3, 1912, indicating at least some degree of acquiescence to Allee's presence.

The court in *Gay* upheld the defendant's conviction for murder in the second degree, finding that the instructions to the jury regarding self-defense had been sufficient and "indeed, favorable to him" (901). The jury had found Gay guilty, in spite of his belief that the deceased and his brother were about to shoot him because each of them had his right hand in his pocket. In fact, they were unarmed. This was one instance where "a reasonable apprehension of danger" was not found to be sufficient to exonerate the defendant.

Finally, since the charge to the jury had contained references to Francisco Gutiérrez Garza, the defense did not want the jurors to dwell on the fate of the old man who had died with his pistol still in the holster while his heart was "almost cut in two" (*San Antonio Express*, August 15, 1912). Therefore, the following admonition was included:

> You are further instructed that the evidence before you relative to the killing of Francisco Gutiérrez Garza can only be considered by you insofar as it may tend to indicate the motive and the intent and purpose of defendant in what he did; and you cannot consider such evidence for any other purpose.

And without further ado, the jury retired to consider the case against Alonzo W. Allee, charged with murder for the homicide of Manuel Gutiérrez García. According to the *Laredo Daily Times* of Tuesday, May 13, 1913, "the case went to the jury shortly before 6 o'clock, after which they partook of their supper, returned to the jury room and shortly after 7 o'clock had reached the verdict of acquittal." The jury verdict, only a torn fragment of which survives, is signed by "N. Worsham, Foreman," the first initial, "J," being torn off.

Alonzo W. Allee was released without a stain on his character, at least as far as the killing of Manuel Gutiérrez was concerned. It was again left to Justo S. Penn to try to explain the results to the readers of the *Times* and the community at large. This was the version of the events that he reported on May 13:

> According to the evidence adduced it was demonstrated that it was evidently a case of self-defense on the part of Allee, who was a cripple at the time as a result of a broken leg. A quarrel had resulted at the ranch house between the three men involved, Allee was knocked down and in the events that followed the two Gutiérrez men were killed.

At least a few of the readers of the *Times* must have marveled at the physical feat necessary to allow a crippled man, knocked down to the floor, to shoot from below—and kill—two healthy, armed men on their feet, emptying his gun while the two were unable to return his fire, with the possible exception of Manuel, who shot at his own feet.

The jury had clearly disregarded Laureano Gutiérrez's testimony. He had given his statement to Justice of the Peace Nicasio Idar on the day after the killings, describing how he had heard a quarrel among the three men. He had heard "the steps of Mr. Allee" as he went to get his gun. This particular description actually gives some credence to Allee's claim (as reported by Justo S. Penn) that he was, if not crippled, at least limping. The limp would have made his footsteps distinctive, so that Laureano could have identified them without being in the same room.

Laureano's statement to the coroner had been that he had observed Alonzo Allee take a gun from his coat and, while Don Francisco remonstrated with him that their business was "not a matter for weapons," Allee had shot Manuel. This was the same story that the jury should have heard, but relating the events to Nicasio Idar in Spanish was not the same thing as being in the jury box, testifying through an interpreter and being cross-examined by Marshall Hicks on the events of nine months before. We do not know how Laureano fared in court; he may have become confused or may have contradicted himself. Or Laureano's testimony may have simply been irrelevant in the eyes of that "all-American panel," the jury.

Nicasio Idar was undoubtedly a much more seasoned witness than the young cowboy Laureano. But Idar's testimony related only to his observations of the bodies and of the scene of the crime. An expert witness on ballistics or medical jurisprudence, such as Dr. H. W. A. Lee, the expert from New Orleans (if that was his function), could easily have contradicted and refuted Idar's conclusions. Idar was, after all, a journalist and a commercial printer by trade, not a forensic expert, and he lacked the scientific background to support his conclusions.

One question that does not seem to have occurred to the jury after hearing Allee's version of the shooting was how a cripple with a broken leg could have made his getaway from the ranch after the killings. According to the newspaper reports, Allee had fled from La Volanta and turned himself in to Deputy Sheriff J. E. Hill at Webb, Texas. How did he get to Webb? He must have had to ride a horse to traverse the brush. If Allee's leg had indeed been broken, it would not have been possible for him to mount a horse, regardless of which leg was broken. He would have needed to put the left foot in the stirrup, and he would have pushed off with the right one to do so, both actions requiring that weight be placed on each leg. In addition, even a newspaper as parsimonious with information as the *Laredo Daily Times* could not have failed to mention a broken leg, had it existed, when it reported Allee's arrest. It seems clear, though, that the jury was not inclined to delve too deeply into inconsistencies and contradictions. They had, as the old saying goes, already made up their minds and did not want to be confused with facts.

Alonzo W. Allee had been acquitted of the murder of Manuel Gutiérrez García, but there still remained pending his indictment for the murder of Francisco Gutiérrez Garza. Would District Attorney Valls now turn his attention to prosecuting the second case against Allee, which presented even more egregious circumstances than the first—the murder of an old man who did not even get to draw his pistol? The answer is no. Before Valls could think of prosecuting Allee again, he had to prosecute a case against Deputy Sheriff Willie Stoner, who was charged with the attempted murder of Manuel García Vigil, the editor of a Laredo Spanish-language newspaper, *El Progreso.*

The Stoner case arose from an incident that occurred on May 7, 1913, the night before Alonzo Allee's trial began. Unlike the Allee indictment, which had languished for some nine months before trial, Stoner found himself on the dock less than one month after his arrest. The Stoner case was called for trial on June 14, 1913, according to the *Laredo Daily Times* of the same day. In the Stoner case, District Attorney Valls again crossed swords with his recent nemesis, Marshall Hicks. Valls was assisted this time by "Greer and Hamilton." Marshall Hicks repeated his ploy of filing for a change of venue, contending that his client could not receive a fair and impartial trial in Webb County because of existing prejudice "precipitated as a result of reports circulated in connection with the bombardment participated in by the two principals in the recent street duel," according to the newspaper report. The motion for a change of venue was denied.

The two principals—Stoner and García Vigil—had indeed engaged in a gun battle in downtown Laredo, almost in front of the offices of the *Laredo Daily Times,* between the *Times* building and Chas. Ross's cantina ("en el espacio que media entre la cantina de Chas Ross y la imprenta del 'Times'"), according to *El Demócrata Fronterizo* of May 10, 1913. Although the participants had exchanged many shots, Stoner came out of it unharmed and García Vigil received only a minor wound. The cause of the dispute had been, according to *El Demócrata Fronterizo,* the ill-advised mixing of political debate with the liquor served at Chas. Ross's cantina.

Since Stoner had come out unscathed and since he was a lawman, the district attorney had charged him with attempted murder—either because he should have set a better example or because he should have been a better shot. In spite of the operatic aspect of the fracas the trial lasted eight days, from June 4 until June 12, when Stoner was found guilty of aggravated assault. The jury assessed his punishment at a fine of one hundred dollars and three months in the county jail, according to the *Times* of June 12, 1913. District Attorney Valls could claim a victory against Marshall Hicks.

On June 25, 1913, the *Laredo Daily Times* ran the following story:

> District Attorney Valls this morning informed the Times reporter that he had dismissed the case pending against Alonzo Allee, who is charged with the killing of Francisco Gutierrez and who at the present term was acquitted by a jury for killing Manuel Gutierrez.
>
> District Attorney Valls says the case was dismissed for good and sufficient reasons, i.e., that he could not expect a different verdict than that of the first trial at a second trial, that the evidence as it pertained to both cases was fully developed at the first trial and that *both cases were practically tried as one* [emphasis added], and that he does not want to put the state and witnesses to the trouble and expense of another trial.

John A. Valls, had indeed filed a motion asking the court to dismiss Cause Number 4874, the State of Texas versus Alonzo W. Allee, on the indictment for the murder of Francisco Gutiérrez Garza. Valls based his motion to dismiss on the reasons given to the newspaper on June 25, and the court granted the motion and entered an order dismissing all charges against Alonzo W. Allee. The interesting point of this transaction is that the order dismissing the case against Allee was filed on June 12, 1913, the same day that District Attorney Valls won a conviction in the Stoner trial, besting his rival, Marshall Hicks. Hicks, however, did not walk away empty-handed on that day: he won the dismissal of the murder charges against his other client, Alonzo Allee.

Marshall Hicks had put his ducks in order from the very beginning of his association with the Allee affair. The outcome of both indictments had been a given since December 1912 when, taking the lead in the case, Hicks had announced that there would be two separate trials and that the trial for killing Manuel Gutiérrez would be held first. Of the two cases, the killing of the son was the most difficult for the prosecution to prove was murder, since Manuel had apparently fired a shot, albeit a useless one. On the other hand, the killing of Manuel Gutiérrez was the only one for which there was a witness, Laureano Gutiérrez. If there had been a second trial, for the murder of the father, the prosecution might have had an easier job swaying the jury because of the age of the victim and the fact that he had not drawn his weapon. However, Marshall Hicks had already managed to impute the motives and the conduct of the younger man to the old one, thereby poisoning the well. John Valls had been accurate when he stated that both cases had been tried in one, although Don Francisco Gutiérrez Garza had never had his day in court.

Manuela García and her daughter, Adela, and Francisca Peña and her seven children, especially sixteen-year-old Virginia and fourteen-year-old Francisco—those who were old enough to understand what had just happened—had seen their hopes for justice not only crushed but also mocked. They had placed their trust in the legal process, and it had failed them. What had seemed at first a serious inquiry to find the truth and a vehicle for righting wrongs turned out to be play-acting. The principal actors had known that. Only the audience had been fooled, as it was meant to be.

Epilogue

AUGUST 1917

On Tuesday, August 7, 1917, the small town of Crystal City, Texas, in Zavala County, some seventy-five miles northwest of Laredo, was awakened to the sounds of a fusillade. A gunfight was in progress that morning on the streets of Crystal City. Crystal City was not an old frontier town of the West, where such incidents were part of the folklore. It was not even an old border town like Laredo, where young cowboys "dressed in white linen" walked the streets, "ready to die" (from the old ballad "The Streets of Laredo"). Crystal City was one of the new settlements that American vision and entrepreneurship had created at the dawn of the twentieth century out of the South Texas brush. It was a modern "planned community," barely ten years old.

David Montejano, in his book *Anglos and Mexicans in the Making of Texas, 1836–1986*, cites James W. Tiller Jr., an economic historian of the Winter Garden, as this area of South Texas was dubbed, to describe the development of the region at the turn of the twentieth century, after the discovery of artesian wells: "Land speculators and men of vision saw that all the ingredients for a successful farming area were present" (106). Ranchers began subdividing their holdings into smaller tracts, which were sold to colonists or "homeseekers" coming from the north to farm. Montejano adds: "The Seven D, Cross S, and Catarina ranches were divided into farms; towns sprang up almost overnight; and the subregion was christened the 'Winter Garden'" (107–108).

Crystal City was one of the new towns created out of the old ranches, the Cross S:

Development strategies were devised by the owner of the Cross S, one of the largest ranches in the United States at the time, and the Pryor ranches; the ranches were subdivided into small farm tracts surrounding the planned communities of Crystal City and La Pryor. Two land speculators, E. J. Buckingham and Carl Groos . . . had purchased all 96,101 acres of the Cross S Ranch in 1905. By 1907 the ranch had been surveyed into sections and each section divided into ten-acre farms. Purchasers of a farm gained title to a town lot in Crystal City. Buckingham and Groos instructed their engineers to place the town near the Nueces River. Extensive advertising encouraged people from all over the United States and a number of foreign countries to settle in Crystal City. The building of the Crystal City and Uvalde Rail-road through La Pryor in 1910 assured access to outside markets and bolstered the county's colonization efforts. (OCHOA 3)

We can only wonder what the transplanted colonists thought and felt that morning of August 7 when they heard the gunfire as they ate their breakfasts or set out to do the day's chores. The scene on main street must have been one of chaos as "the air resounded with shots, a pitched battle ensuing and people running from the streets to avoid being hit by stray bullets," as the *Laredo Daily Times* reported later that day. The results of the battle of Crystal City were several wounded men, one mortally so, and one man killed as he walked away from the carnage he had inflicted: Alonzo W. Allee.

The headline on the front page of the *Laredo Daily Times* on August 7, 1917, read: ALLEE WAS KILLED BY BUTLER TODAY. The following paragraphs told the story:

> As a result of a general shooting scrape that took place on the streets of Crystal City this morning at 8 o'clock, when the entire population of that little town was thrown into a state of excitement by the promiscuous firing of firearms, Alonzo Allee, a well known stockman, is dead. One of the Butler brothers of Crystal City is so seriously wounded that he is not expected to live; another of the Butlers was wounded in the arm, and Burt Mitchell, a stockman, had his left arm shot off.
>
> Allee was killed after he walked away after shooting the two Butlers and Mitchell by a young son of one of the Butlers,

who had run to his home and secured a 30:30 Winchester and followed Allee to a drugstore and shot him in the back, the bullet going through Allee's heart and causing instant death, the man falling dead on the drugstore floor.

The description of Alonzo Allee walking away, leaving three wounded men behind, is reminiscent of the scene on the train where Alfred Y. Allee, after shooting the Bowen brothers of Cotulla (the lawyer and the editor), "coolly walked out of the coach, knocking the empty shells from his cartridge belt" (Ludeman 117). Alonzo, like his father, knew that he had nothing to fear from the men he had felled and that he could turn his back on them. However, he had overlooked Butler's young son, who became the avenger of his father.

The *Carrizo Springs Javelin*, a weekly newspaper from neighboring Dimmit County, also carried the story of the shoot-out on Friday, August 10, 1917, and reported that in the interim since August 7 Sidney Butler, who had received serious wounds to the stomach and lungs, had died a short time after being taken to San Antonio for treatment. The *Javelin* story included background details on the cause of the "affray:"

> The affray seems to have been the result of bad blood which has existed between the Mitchell cattle outfit and that of Allee for some months. The day previous to the shooting there was a personal difficulty between Mitchell and Allee, followed by the shooting the following morning.

The *Laredo Daily Times* described the motive for the fight between Allee and Mitchell and Butler as arising "over a dispute regarding some pasturage matters." And in 1971 Alonzo Allee's son, A. Y. Allee, told an interviewer that in 1918—not 1917—his father had been killed in Crystal City "in a cattle dispute" (Pattie, "A. Y. Allee" 43). The impression we are left with from these allusions is of a festering range war between Mitchell's "cattle outfit," to which the Butlers were attached, and Allee's. But which was Allee's?

One question that comes to mind after reading the previous accounts is, What had Alonzo Allee been doing since the summer of 1913, after he was acquitted of the murder of Manuel Gutiérrez and the charges against him were dismissed in the killing of Don Francisco Gutiérrez? Obviously, he had quitted the premises at La Volanta after he had killed the owners there. By 1913, according to his son, A. Y. Allee, Alonzo was in Zavala County (presumably, after his legal troubles had been satisfactorily resolved). The same interviewer reported: "When Alonzo got a chance to lease the west side of the Cross S Ranch near Crystal City [for ten cents an acre] in 1913 he moved 1500 head of cattle there" (Pattie, "A. Y. Allee" 43). Apparently, not all of the Cross S Ranch had been subdivided and sold in ten-acre tracts to farmers; the "west side" was still being used to pasture cattle by Alonzo Allee.

When A. J. Landrum had leased La Volanta from Don Francisco Gutiérrez, he (Landrum) had agreed to pay fifteen cents an acre as rent. And when Alonzo Allee had sent a lease payment to Manuel Gutiérrez, the check had been for $450.26, and it purported to cover six months rent, from April to October of 1912, an amount reflecting fifteen cents an acre. Yet, when he leased the west side of the Cross S Ranch, Allee was paying only ten cents an acre. Of course, we don't know how much land Allee was leasing at this time, but it is interesting that he was able to lease this land for one-third less than he had paid the year before at La Volanta. Perhaps the land in Zavala County was inferior to that in Webb County; or perhaps Allee had struck a different kind of deal with his new landlord to explain the lower rent.

It was during this time in Zavala County that Alonzo W. Allee was appointed a Special Texas Ranger. On July 10, 1916, A. W. Allee voluntarily enrolled as a private in the Ranger Force of the State of Texas for a period of two years. On July 17, 1916, the adjutant general of the state commissioned Allee as a Special Ranger with the proviso that it was "without expense to the state." From the "Enrollment and Oath of Service" form we learn that A. W. Allee was born in Goliad County, Texas, that in July of 1916 he was thirty-eight years and two months old, and that he listed his occupation as "stockman." He is also described as being five feet nine and three-quarter inches tall, of fair complexion, with blue-gray eyes and sandy brown hair.

Also commissioned as a Special Ranger at the same time as Allee was Sidney Butler, Allee's future victim.

If the state did not furnish the Special Rangers with "bounty, pay, subsistence and other expenses" (the line relating to payment is crossed out), then it seems curious that Allee and Butler—or anybody else, for that matter—would have enrolled under those conditions. Naturally there was payment and, as we have said before, it usually came from the Texas Cattle Raisers Association, as it was known then. This proposition is reinforced by Alonzo Allee's son, Warren P. Allee, who himself retired from employment with the Texas and Southwestern Cattle Raisers Association after forty-two years of service. Warren P. Allee remembered that when he was eighteen years or so, he found some of his father's belongings in a trunk and that there he "noticed a little book that had been put out by the Cattle Raisers Association." He added: "It may have been one of the first they ever published" (Pattie, "To the Letter" 100).

Alonzo Allee did not remain a Special Ranger for very long. He resigned on April 25, 1917, less than a year after he had signed on for two years. We do not know what Allee's duties were in those few months that he belonged to the Special Rangers, but, as we have said before, the Cattle Raisers Association maintained its own police force to investigate and prosecute cattle thieves. The Special Rangers were that police force, commissioned by the state but paid for by the Cattle Raisers.

Apparently, appointments such as Alonzo Allee had had were numerous, leading one historian to remark: "The appointment of hundreds of Special Rangers cheapened the badge" (Weiss 637).

Out of this tenuous connection of Alonzo Allee with the Rangers—and of Alfred Allee being deputized to kill Brack Cornett, the bank robber—was born the legend of the dynasty of Allee Texas Rangers. Like all legends, many of the details are hidden in clouds of mystery. It is a mystery, for example, why Alonzo Allee's sons were unable to recollect accurately the year of their father's death when surely they had visited his grave and seen the headstone with the date of his death: August 7, 1917. A. Y. Allee gave the year of his father's death as 1918 (Pattie, "A. Y. Allee" 43). Warren P. Allee related: "I was born in Crystal City . . . on December 16, 1915. At that time my father had an extensive ranching operation near Crystal City. At the time of his death, I was only three or four years old" (Pattie, "To the Letter" 100).

The exact nature of the dispute over cattle or over pasturage that led to Allee's death also remains a mystery after all these years, as does the identity of Allee's employer, which the newspapers never revealed but whose existence is almost certain. Alonzo Allee resembled the pilot fish that in the ocean announces the presence of sharks. Likewise, in the brush country of southwest Texas, Allee's presence can be viewed as indicating the presence of John R. Blocker not far away. Alonzo Allee had leased part of the Cross S Ranch where, it turns out, Blocker had cattle operations. Perhaps Blocker had been the landlord who had given

Allee a favorable lease in exchange for Allee's services. Those services may have led to his death.

Less than three weeks after Allee's death a notice appeared in the *Carrizo Springs Javelin* of August 24. The notice, from John Blocker to the public, read:

NOTICE TO RANCHERS

Owing to rumors in circulation, I will consider it a favor and a duty for all ranchmen in this vicinity to come or send a representative to be at the old headquarters Cross S Ranch Monday evening the 3rd of September for the purpose of rounding up the pasture so everyone can see if he has any cattle in this pasture and can get them out. I will have a camp outfit at the ranch to feed all that come during the work. [Signed] J. R. Blocker.

In all probability, this was the "cattle dispute" that Alonzo's son alluded to and the disagreement regarding "some pasturage matters" that the Laredo newspaper reported as the cause for the violence that killed Sidney Butler and Alonzo Allee. "Rumors in circulation" in Zavala County were likely to be that "Allee's outfit" had been stealing cattle, and now, after Allee's death, Blocker was calling for a truce.

Blocker quite possibly regretted the loss of his loyal henchman. According to the *Javelin*, many people—besides Allee's family—did. Whether this was an accurate observation or simply a case of the pious "nothing but good of the dead," we have no way of knowing; but the August 10 issue of the *Javelin* recounted: "The funeral of Mr. Allee was held in Crystal City Wednesday [August 8] and was one of the largest funerals ever held here. The dead man had a host of friends who mourn his untimely death sincerely."

August 8, 1917, was only one week short of the five-year anniversary of the unusual and well-attended double funeral held in Laredo's San Agustín Cathedral for Francisco Gutiérrez Garza and his son, Manuel Gutiérrez García, dead by the gun of Alonzo W. Allee. Now it had been his turn to die by the gun.

Alonzo Allee's violent end must have brought back the events of 1913 to both his prosecutor, John Anthony Valls, and his defense counsel, Marshall Hicks. Since 1913 the careers of both men had continued to prosper in their chosen fields. Valls had continued to be reelected, and looking ahead to 1918, he did not even have an opponent. Valls had also acquired valuable real estate investments in Laredo.

Marshall Hicks still practiced law in South Texas and was the political fixer of choice in high places. In 1913 his reputation reached all the way to Mexico City. That was when he became "attorney for the Mexican government during the administration of Victoriano Huerta," according to an article in the *Austin American* ("Who's Who"). Victoriano Huerta, known in Mexican history as "the usurper," had brought about the assassination in Mexico City of President Madero in 1913 while Laredo celebrated George Washinton's birthday. Unfortunately for Hicks, Huerta's regime was short-lived, and by August 1914 he had been ousted from power (Fehrenbach 518).

Marshall Hicks maintained a strong presence in Laredo, and his frequent visits there were duly noted by the newspaper. On February 17, 1918, an item in the *Times* read: "Marshall Hicks, esq., of San Antonio is here on a business visit." The following month, on March 6, the *Times* reported:

> The Times publishes in another column notice of the new law
> partnership of Hicks, Phelps, Dickson and Bobbit. . . . Messrs.
> Marshall and Yale Hicks are well known to the readers of the
> Times and need no commendation from us, having being associ-
> ated with the legal business of Laredo and Southwest Texas for
> more than 25 years. . . . The Laredo offices of the new firm are
> in the Valls Building in Laredo.

Marshall Hicks died in 1930 at the age of sixty-five and left no immediate survivors except his brother Yale and two sisters ("Marshall Hicks," *Texas Pioneer*). John Valls died in August 1941. He had never married and had worked until the end—but not as the district attorney of Webb County. In 1938 he had left that post to become district judge of the Forty-ninth Judicial District, succeeding his old friend Judge John F. Mullally (Green, "John Valls" 24).

With the passing of the two friendly antagonists, not many were left to remember Alonzo Allee's trial for the murders of Francisco and Manuel Gutiérrcz. The families of the victims, of course, did not forget. For them the death of Alonzo Allee had come five years too late.

AFTERWORD

At best, people who write about old crimes have to rely on logic.
— *FRANCES AND RICHARD LOCKRIDGE, Murder within Murder*

Logic is a poor substitute for firsthand knowledge, but sometimes that is all we have. In writing this book I have had to rely on logic, as well as on newspaper accounts, second-hand memories, and a few surviving legal documents, to create a picture of how and why the events narrated here happened, or must have happened.

Because the trial resulted in an acquittal, the testimony of the witnesses was not preserved as it is when an appeal follows a guilty verdict. While researching the trial, I had feverishly hoped that somewhere I would discover a treasure trove—the trial notes of Seb Wilcox, the court reporter. I did not, but I was comforted in my disappointment by a retired court reporter who told me that in the early days of his career he had been a "pen writer." Before the advent of the steno machine, court reporters took down testimony by pen in either of two systems of shorthand, Gregg or Pittman. Shorthand today must be akin to a dead language, but there is at least the possibility of deciphering ancient Greek. However, according to my source, many court reporters in the old days developed their own shorthand, referred to as "eclectic" shorthand, and when those reporters died or were unable to transcribe their notes, all hope of translation was gone.

Seb Wilcox died in 1959, but, although he donated his extensive collection of papers on Laredo to the library of Saint Mary's University in San Antonio, Wilcox, ever discreet, did not include his court reporter notes among them. The retired court reporter assuaged my disappointment by pointing out that even had I found those notes, most likely I would not have been able to read them.

My job, then, became one of reconstructing testimony and of explaining events. Therefore, with a few exceptions the testimony of the witnesses, unless reported by the newspapers of the day, must be inferred from the results it accomplished. Likewise, much of the motivation of the main participants can only be understood by examining the circumstances surrounding their actions, and this I have done by presenting elements of the personal histories of the protagonists, as well as the societal forces that shaped them.

The essential facts of this story are not in dispute. After carefully considering those facts, I reached conclusions that seemed to me inescapable. If reasonable minds differ on some of these conclusions, so be it. It suffices if, almost one hundred years later, a particular miscarriage of justice is righted in some reader's mind.

Beatriz de la Garza
Austin, Texas

WORKS CITED

BOOKS AND ARTICLES

Bushick, Frank H. *Glamorous Days.* San Antonio: Naylor Co., 1934.

Calderón, Roberto R. "Mexican Politics in the American Era, 1846–1900: Laredo, Texas." Ph.D. diss., UCLA, 1993.

Cearly, Violet. "Penn, James Saunders." *The New Handbook of Texas.* Austin: Texas State Historical Assoc., 1996.

Cribbet, John E. *Principles of the Law of Property.* 2d ed. Mineola NY: Foundation Press, 1975.

Cumberland, Charles C. *Mexican Revolution: Genesis under Madero.* Austin: U of Texas P, 1952.

Da Camara, Kathleen. *Laredo on the Rio Grande.* San Antonio: Naylor Co., 1949.

Dailey, Henry W. "Alfred Allee Had Eventful Career." *Frontier Times* 10.7 (n.d.): 326–330. Reprint *Kenedy Advance,* n.d.

Egloff, Fred R. "Lawmen and Gunmen: A Contrasting View of Old West Peace Officers in Kansas and Texas." *Journal of the West* 34.1 (1995): 19–26.

Escriche, Joaquín. *Diccionario razonado de legislación y jurisprudencia.* vol. 1. Madrid: n.p., 1874.

Falvella, James W. *A Souvenir Album of Laredo, the Gateway to Mexico.* Laredo TX: n.p., 1916.

———. *Souvenir Program of the Seventeenth George Washington Celebration.* Laredo TX: n.p., 1916.

Fehrenbach, T. R. *Fire and Blood: A History of Mexico.* New York: Macmillan, 1973.

Garza-Falcón, Leticia. *Gente Decente: A Borderlands Response to the Rhetoric of Dominance.* Austin: U of Texas P, 1998.

Green, Stan. *John Valls and the Laredo Bar.* Border Studies. Laredo TX: Texas A&M International U, 1991.

———. *An Overview of Rural Webb County.* Laredo TX: Webb County Heritage Foundation, 1992.

———, ed. *Border Biographies.* 2 vols. 2d ed. Laredo TX: Texas A&M International U, 1993.

General Directory of the City of Laredo, 1900. Laredo: Arguindegui and McDonell, 1900.

Guide to Spanish and Mexican Land Grants. Austin: Texas General Land Office, 1988.

Hinojosa, Gilberto Miguel. *A Borderlands Town in Transition: Laredo, 1755–1870.* College Station: Texas A&M UP, 1983.

History of the Cattlemen of Texas. Reprint 1914. Introd. Harwood P. Hinton. Austin: Texas State Historical Assoc., 1991.

Izaguirre, Beatriz C. *Zapata County Folklore.* Zapata TX: Zapata County Historical Society, 1983.

Jackson, Jack. *Los Mesteños: Spanish Ranching in Texas, 1721–1821.* College Station: Texas A&M UP, 1986.

Jacobs, Janet. "Cattle Rustling Making a Comeback." *Austin American-Statesman* 24 Nov. 2000: B1-2.

Leffler, John, and Christopher Long. "Webb County." *The New Handbook of Texas.* Austin: Texas State Historical Assoc., 1996.

Limón, José E. "El Primer Congreso Mexicanista de 1911: A Precursor to Contemporary Chicanismo." *Aztlán* 5.1–2 (1974): 85–117.

Loaeza, Guadalupe. *Las niñas bien.* Mexico, D.F.: Cal y Arena, 1994.

Lott, Virgil, and Mercurio Martínez. *The Kingdom of Zapata.* 1953. Austin: Eakin Press, 1983.

Ludeman, Annette Martin. *LaSalle County: South Texas Brush Country, 1856–1975.* Texas County History Series. N.p.: Nortex Press, 1975.

"Marshall Hicks." *Texas Pioneer.* Aug.–Sept. 1930. Vertical Files, Center for American History, U of Texas, Austin.

Marshall, Larry, T. C. Richardson, and Dick Wilson. "Texas and Southwestern Cattle Raisers Association." *The New Handbook of Texas.* Austin: Texas State Historical Assoc., 1996.

Miller, Thomas Lloyd. *The Public Lands of Texas, 1519–1970.* Norman: U of Oklahoma P, 1971.

Montejano, David. *Anglos and Mexicans in the Making of Texas, 1836–1986.* Austin: U of Texas P, 1987.

Los municipios de Nuevo León. Colección Enciclopedia de los municipios de México. Monterrey Mex: n.p., 1988.

The New Handbook of Texas. 6 vols. Austin: Texas State Historical Assoc., 1996.

Novinger, Tracy. *Intercultural Communication: A Practical Guide.* Austin: U of Texas P, 2001.

Ochoa, Ruben E. "Zavala County." *The Handbook of Texas Online.* General Libraries of the U of Texas at Austin and the Texas State Historical Assoc. 15 Feb. 1999. http://www.tsha.utexas.edu/handbook/online.

Pattie, Jane. "A. Y. Allee: The Man and the Legend." *Texas Parade,* Dec. 1971, 42–46.

———. "To the Letter of the Law." *The Cattleman,* Oct. 1988, 100–112.

Rutherford, John. *Mexican Society during the Revolution: A Literary Approach.* Oxford: Clarendon-Oxford UP, 1971.

Schreiner, Charles III. *A Pictorial History of the Texas Rangers.* Mountain Home TX: Y-O Press, 1969.

Scott, Florence Johnson. *Historical Heritage of the Lower Rio Grande.* 1937, Waco TX: Texian Press, 1970.

A Shared Experience. 2d ed. Austin: Los Caminos del Rio Heritage Project and Texas Historical Commission, 1994.

Stumberg, George Wilfred. "Defense of Person and Property under Texas Criminal Law." *Texas Law Review* 21 (1942–43): 17–35.

Tarver, E. R. *Laredo, the Gateway between the United States and Mexico: An Illustrated Description of the Future City of the Great Southwest.* Laredo TX: n.p., 1889.

Texas Almanac and State Industrial Guide, 1984–85. Dallas: A. H. Belo Corp., 1983.

Texas Family Land Heritage Registry, 1980. Austin: Texas Department of Agriculture, 1980.

Thompson, Jerry. *Laredo: A Pictorial History.* Norfolk VA: Donning Co., 1986.

A Twentieth Century History of Southwest Texas. 2 vols. Chicago: Lewis Publishing, 1907.

Webb, Walter Prescott. *The Texas Rangers: A Century of Frontier Defense.* 2d ed. Austin: U of Texas P, 1998.

Weiss. Harold J., Jr. "The Texas Rangers Revisited: Old Themes and New Viewpoints." *Southwestern Historical Quarterly* 97.4 (Apr. 1994): 621–640.

Wharton, Clarence R. *Texas under Many Flags.* 5 vols. Chicago: American Historical Society, 1930.

"Who's Who in Texas and Why—Marshall Hicks." *Austin American* 1917(?). Vertical Files, Center for American History, U of Texas, Austin.

Wilcox, Seb S. "The Story of Dimmit County, Texas: A Paper Given before the Rotary Club of Carrizo Springs, September 9, 1937." Typescript. Texas State Library and Archives, Austin.

Wilkinson, J. B. *Laredo and the Rio Grande Frontier.* Austin: Jenkins Publishing, 1975.

Woodward, M. K., and Robert Hobbs. *Cases and Materials on Texas Land Titles.* Austin TX: Sterling Swift Publishing, 1975.

Worley, Alicia Consuelo. "The Life of John Anthony Valls." Master's thesis, Texas College of Arts and Industries, 1954.

Young, Elliot. "Deconstructing *La Raza:* Identifying the *Gente Decente* of Laredo, 1904–1911." *Southwestern Historical Quarterly* 98.2 (Oct. 1994): 226–259.

———. "Penn, Justo Sabor." *The New Handbook of Texas.* Austin: Texas State Historical Assoc., 1996.

———. "Red Men, Princess Pocahontas, and George Washington: Harmonizing Race Relations in Laredo at the Turn of the Century." *Western Historical Quarterly* 29.1 (1998): 49–85.

NEWSPAPERS

Austin American, Austin, TX. 1917 (?).
Austin American-Statesman, Austin, TX. 2000.
Brownsville Herald, Brownsville, TX. 1915, 1916, 1918.
Carrizo Springs Javelin, Carrizo Springs, TX. 1917.
La Crónica, Laredo, TX. 1910, 1911.
El Demócrata Fronterizo, Laredo, TX. 1912, 1913.
Laredo Daily Times, Laredo, TX. 1912, 1913, 1917, 1918.
Laredo Times, Laredo, TX. 1981.
Laredo Weekly Times, Laredo, TX. 1912.
San Antonio Express, San Antonio, TX. 1912.
San Antonio Light, San Antonio, TX. 1912.

ARCHIVAL COLLECTIONS

Archivo Municipal. Nueva Ciudad Guerrero, Tamaulipas, México.
Center for American History. University of Texas at Austin.
Center for Legal History. State Bar of Texas, Austin, TX.
District Court Civil and Criminal Records, 1848–1920. UT Pan American Library, Edinburg, TX.
Laredo Public Library. Luciano Guajardo Historical Collection. Laredo, TX.
Spanish Archives. General Land Office of Texas. Austin, TX.
Texas State Library and Archives. Austin, TX.
Webb County Heritage Foundation. Laredo, TX.
Webb County Land Records. County Clerk's Office, Laredo, TX.
Webb County Probate Records. County Clerk's Office, Laredo, TX.

ACKNOWLEDGMENTS

This book was made possible with the encouragement and assistance of various persons. First and foremost, my gratitude goes to Sylvia Lozano Trzaskoma, great-granddaughter and granddaughter, respectively, of Don Francisco Gutiérrez and Manuel Gutiérrez, and to her husband, Lt. Gen. Richard J. Trzaskoma, USAF (Ret.), who generously shared their research, their memories, and their photographs with me. Many thanks too and my admiration to Dick Trzaskoma for his wizardry with the Internet.

I am likewise grateful for the assistance I received from the persons at the sites where my research led me. In Nueva Ciudad Guerrero, Tamaulipas, México: Mil gracias a María del Carmen González, quien tiene a su cuidado el Archivo Municipal de Ciudad Guerrero, y al Sr. Don Juan A. García Pérez por encaminarme hacia esa valiosa fuente de datos. In Laredo, Texas: Mr. Joe Moreno Jr., Special Collections Librarian, and the staff of the Laredo Public Library; the staff of the Webb County Heritage Foundation; and the staff of the Webb County Clerk's Office. In Austin: Margo Gutiérrez and Adán Benavides of the Benson Latin American Collection of the University of Texas at Austin; the staff of the Center for American History at UT Austin; John Anderson of the State Library and Archives; Galen Greaser of the Spanish Archives at the Texas General Land Office; Abby Wood of the State Preservation Board; and the staff of the Center for Legal History of the State Bar of Texas.

I am also grateful to Mrs. J. Conrad Dunagan and the staff of Dunagan Enterprises, of Monahans, Texas, and to Mr. Ed Idar Jr., of San Antonio, Texas, for sharing family documents and photographs. My thanks also to Professor Leticia Garza-Falcón; to J. Gilberto Quezada; and to Dr. Mario L. Sánchez, formerly with the Texas Historical Commission, for directing me to valuable research sources.

Likewise, to all those helpful persons in various places, such as Southwestern University in Georgetown, Texas, who patiently and cheerfully answered my questions—thank you.

Finally, I want to express my appreciation to the academic readers, whose comments and suggestions for my manuscript helped to make this a better book.

INDEX

García, Eusebio, 103, 104
García, José María, 8
García, P. N., 95
García, Virginia, 8, 11, 19
García de Gutiérrez, Manuela, 3, 7–10, 102, 120
García Vigil, Manuel, 118
Garza Galán, Col. Andrés, 87
General Land Office, Texas, 22
gente decente, defined, 57–59
George Washington's Birthday Celebration, Laredo, 83–86
Gould, Jay, 2
grand jury, Allee case, 43, 47–48, 61
Groos, Carl, 122
Guerra, Macedonio, 103, 104
Gutiérrez, Bernabé, 3
Gutiérrez, Estanislao, 5
Gutiérrez, Francisco, 5, 48, 51, 52–54, 101
Gutiérrez, José Manuel, 53
Gutiérrez, Julián, 5, 22, 23, 48, 52–54, 102
Gutiérrez, Laureano, 5, 48, 49–51, 53–54, 67, 101–102, 108, 112, 113, 117
Gutiérrez, Pilar, 5
Gutiérrez, Virginia, 10, 11, 26, 27, 120
Gutiérrez de Flores, Adela, 3, 8, 120
Gutiérrez García, Manuel: charge to Allee jury, 110–114; death, 16–19; estate of, 5, 45; family life, 3, 8–10; funeral, 25; indictment of killer, 48; land ownership, 22, 32; lease problems, 11; parents, 3, 8; prominence of, 16; trial, 91; trips, 11, 12, 14, 20, 115; verdict, 116; wounds, description of, 26, 55
Gutiérrez Garza, Francisco: *alcalde primero*, 5, 18, 19; ancestral home, 3; binational, 3; case, 91, 119; children, 8; education, 52–53; estate of, 5, 32; funeral, 25; killed, 15–17; killer indicted, 48; last words, 49–50, 57; La Volanta, owner, 5; leave of absence, 5;

new lease, 12; parents, 53; prominence of, 16; ranches, 4, 5, 9; special instructions to jury, 114–116; state land purchases, 5, 22; wounds, 26, 56, 116
Gutiérrez Peña, Francisco, 10, 27, 33, 120

Hamilton, Arthur Claude, 62, 65, 108
Hamilton and Mann (law firm), 68
Hearst, Cleave, 42
Heights District (Laredo), 100
Henrichsen, R. L., 48, 77
Henry, Joe, 43
Henderson, Mrs. Lem, 82
Hernandez case, 96–97
Herrera, Alicia, 1, 98
Herrera, J. F., 95
Hewitt, Jesse, 93, 95
Hicks, Marshall: change of venue, Allee case, 77–80, 83; change of venue, Stoner case, 118; curriculum vitae, 27, 39; death, 127; dismissal, second Allee case, 119; represented Allee, 28; represented Huerta government, 127; special instructions to Allee jury, 113; supported Judge Mullally's appointment, 110; trial strategy, 113, 119–120
Hicks, Yale, 108, 110, 127
Hicks and Teargarden, 39, 75
Hill, J. E., 21, 30, 31, 43, 102
Hill, Will T., 37
Hobbs, W. H., 105
Hogg, James (Governor), 27, 76
home section, 23. *See also* land scrip
homeseekers, 121
householder, 94. *See also* juror
Huerta, Victoriano, 89, 127

Idar, Clemente, 81
Idar, Eduardo, 81
Idar, Jovita, 81
Idar, Nicasio, 20, 25, 48, 50, 52, 54–56, 80–81, 102, 103, 117

Improved Order of Red Men, 83–84
international bridge, Laredo, 6, 7, 88
International and Great Northern Railway, 2, 21, 27, 86
Ireland, John (Governor), 97, 99

Jim Hogg County, 4, 21
Johnson, H. C., 105
Johnson, R. M., 93, 95. *See also* jury
Jones, W. W., 48
judges, Texas, 109
juror, Texas, 94–95
jury, Allee case, 94, 95, 99, 100–101, 110–116
jury commission, 92
justifiable homicide, 106–108

Karnes County, 31, 33
Kyle, Charles Vigil, 11

La Crónica, 46, 50, 80, 81, 82
La Leona, 18
land grants, 4, 5
land scrip, 22, 23
Landrum, A. J., 5, 11, 13, 79, 105, 115
Landrum, Bessie, 11
land titles, South Texas, 3, 4
Lane, Colonel E. R., 36
Lanham, S. W. T. (Governor), 62, 110
La Posta, 6
La Rebelde, 46
Laredo, jurisdiction of, 4; population of, 43, 44, 93
Laredo Immigration Society, 2, 46
LaSalle County, 31, 32, 33, 35, 37
Las Mujeres Creek, 50
Las Mujeres Ranch, 49, 50
La Volanta Ranch, 11–13, 15–16, 17, 20–23, 49, 56, 59, 124
leaseholds law, 12–13
Lee, Dr. H. W. A., 91, 104, 105, 117
Levy, Meyer M., 23
Levytansky, G. J., 29, 80, 105
Leyendecker, Joe, 43
Leyendecker, John Z., 44
Leyendecker, P. P., 42

Ligarde, H., 83
literacy, English, 94. *See also* juror
Lowry, Dr. W. E., 103, 104, 105

Mackin, Sam, 95, 99. *See also* jury
Madero, Francisco (President), 1, 3, 73, 74, 86, 87, 89, 127
Madero, Gustavo, 1
mail, to Laredo, 6
Mann, T. C., 12
manslaughter, 110, 113
Martin, Geo. M., 39, 105
Martin, J. C., 43
Masterson, B. W., 43
Maverick County, 40
McComb, Robert, 83
McKenzie, Sam (also McKinzie, McKinsie), 20, 25, 42, 103, 105–106
Medrano, Atanacio, 103
Medrano, Pedro, 67, 103, 105
Medrano, Ramón, 66, 67, 70, 103
"Mexican," usage defined, 96
Mexican National Railroad, 2, 86, 88
Mexican Revolution, 86–90
Mexico City, 1, 2, 82
Mier, Tamaulipas, Mexico, 2
Mitchell, Burt, 122, 123
Monterrey, Nuevo León, Mexico, 1
Mueller, Virginia Josephine, 97
Mullally, Judge John F., 42–43, 61–62, 83, 84, 109–110, 110–112
municipal election, 1912, Ciudad Guerrero, Tamaulipas, 18
Municipality of Ciudad Guerrero, 17–18

Neutrality Laws, 73, 90
Nuestra Señora del Refugio Parish, 8
Nuevo Santander, 3, 46

Oliver, A. P., 105
Orden Caballeros de Honor, 81
original grantees, 3–4
Orozco, Pascual, 1, 74

Treviño, José, 95
Treviño, Leonardo and Teodoro, 23

Ursuline convent school, 10, 27

Valdez, Nicanor, 87
Valls, John Anthony: absent at final arguments, 108; biography, 62, 63–65, 72; Compton case, 29; death, 127; dismissed second Allee case, 119; election, 1912, 61–62; famed orator, 108–109; followed Judge Mullally, 127; opinion, attorney general, 68–70; opposed change of venue, 78–79; *porfirista*, 65, 72; prosecuted Stoner, 118; real estate, 127
Valls, William and Evelina, 64
Vandervoort, F., 40, 48
Vandervoort, J., 39
Vásquez Borrego, Don José, 71
venires, Allee case, 63, 66, 91, 92–95
Villegas, Joaquín, 45, 46
Villegas, Leopoldo, 43, 45, 46, 48
Villegas, Lorenzo, 46

Villegas, Quintín, 46
Villegas de Magnón, Leonor, 46
voter, qualified, 94

Webb County, 5, 24, 39, 40, 43, 44, 47, 61, 76, 93
Webb, Texas, 2, 21
Weber, G. R., 93, 95, 100. *See also* jury
Wilcox, Seb, 40, 62, 63
Wilson, Woodrow (President), 61
Winn, John, 105
Winter Garden area, 121
Woodward, R. P., 95. *See also* jury
Worsham, J. N., 93, 95. *See also* jury
Wright, Will, 42
writ of attachment, 103–104

Yates, Sam, 105, 112
Young, W. N., 43

Zapata, Emiliano, 1
Zapata County, 3, 6–7, 21, 23, 39, 112
Zavala County, 121, 124, 126